Some Preterism, Some Futu— Some Confusion
Edomites fight Judahites
" became "Jews" p5—
2520 years to 1917 p75
Moslems symbolic of sun + m—
85% of Jews are not Israel p—

Olivet

Being "strong enough" instead of being "counted worthy" P99

Prophecies

Capt says no Scriptural ground for supporting todays
popular "rapture" and "left behind" doctrines.

E. Raymond Capt M.A., A.I.A., F.S.A. Scot

Table of Contents

The Glory of Prophecy

No subject is more fascinating than prophecy. Particularly fascinating is the Divine forecast regarding the future of God's people and of the world. Because prophecy deals with the future, it is perhaps the most difficult of all Biblical subjects to understand. Only until fulfillment is complete can one comprehend the marvelous accuracy of the utterances of the prophets of the Lord.

Prophecy itself, is often couched in such terms that it is impossible to understand many of its details until the time arrives for fulfillment. Even then, it may not be clear until later when events can be reviewed in retrospect. Prophecy has not been given to men to make them prophets, but rather for the purpose of confirming God's Word and thus to know and recognize the truth.

The prophecies of the Bible have two functions: to manifest the glory of God and to give guidance and warning to men. These functions are given expression again and again in the Scriptures. The first function is expressed in Isaiah 46: 9-10: "For I am God, and there is none else; I am God, and there is none like me, declaring the end from the beginning, and from ancient times the things that are not yet done, saying, My council shall stand, and I will do all my pleasure."

The second function is disclosed in Amos 3:7: "Surely, the Lord God will do nothing but he revealeth his secret unto his servants the prophets," and in Daniel 12:10: "None of the wicked shall understand, but the wise shall understand." Although all prophecy discloses the glory of God, there are some prophecies which show this to a greater degree than others. The prophecies deal with two types of material. Some of the prophecies are wholly concerned in describing future happenings and events in the physical world of nature. Others are to foretell what men, either as individuals or in groups will do.

The importance of prophecy was recognized by the Apostle Peter who, speaking of the glory of the transfiguration when on the Mount where he was an eye witness of the glory of the coming of the Lord, wrote: "We have also a more sure word of prophecy; whereunto ye do well that ye take heed, as unto a light that shineth in a dark place, until the day dawn, and the day star arise in your hearts: Knowing this first, that no prophecy of the scripture is of any private interpretation. For the prophecy came not in old time by the will of man; but holy men of God spake as they were moved by the Holy Ghost." (II Peter 1:19-21)

Prophecy can only be fully understood when it is read in the light of the historical events that are predicted. For this reason, many Bible scholars who are deficient in this field have accepted the so-called many fulfilled prophecies have not yet had their fulfillment. Consequently, so many supposedly unfulfilled prophecies have been relegated to the future that a congestion of future events exist that defies being put together in any coherent sequence.

In His prophecies Jesus used symbolic language. Because symbols have been subjected to speculative interpretations by modern influential Bible scholars, confusion and controversy hinder a clear understanding of what Jesus really intended to convey to His listeners. However, when it is recognized that each symbol in the Scriptures carried the same meaning throughout the entire Book, the hindrance is removed.

This study is confined to the predictions Jesus made to His disciples that came to be known as the "Olivet Prophecies," and their fulfillment. The scriptures provide three versions of these discourses; the accounts of Matthew, Mark and Luke. The three accounts recording the words of Jesus differ in detail and emphasis, in the same manner as three witnesses to an event differ in reporting what each saw and heard. However, when all three accounts are correlated and read in the light of the historical events that are predicted, we get a complete, but somewhat different view from what many Bible scholars teach, resulting in confusion to an understanding of the "last days."

Only by consulting each of the three versions together with the recorded history of the period can a complete account of the prophecies by obtained. In doing so, it is important not to give an application of any prophecy an entirely different application from that of another writer.

The Olivet Prophecies

Two days before His betrayal and crucifixion, Jesus sat with His disciples upon the Mount of Olives and talked with them about the future. He had already tried to explain to them that He would need to leave them; how He would be betrayed, tried for His life, put to death and then would come back to life again. Had He cared to be explicit, He might have disclosed that the place where His feet would leave the ground in His ascension into Heaven was the very spot where He sat with them on the Mount of Olives.

Earlier that day Jesus had visited the Temple with His disciples when one remarked to Him, "Master, see what manner of stones and what buildings are here! And Jesus answering said unto him, Seest thou these great buildings? there shall not be left one stone upon another, that shall not be thrown down." (Mark 13:1-2) Jesus in His Divine Wisdom foresaw the legions of Rome marching upon Jerusalem and Titus adding another city to his list of conquered cities. This was to occur less than forty years from the time they were sitting together.

The disciples seemingly accepted the fact that Jerusalem was going to soon be destroyed and believed the prophecy to take place in their own time. However, they were also curious about the details of the end-days which would precede the establishment of the Kingdom of God upon the earth and the return of Jesus as King with a new Jerusalem to take the place of the old. The prophets of their Scriptures had testified of this Kingdom which was to be established upon the earth.

Daniel had described it as a "Stone Kingdom" which would smash all other existing kingdoms. The minds of the disciples had been steeped in the words of the prophets, who had voiced so many times the covenants and purposes of God in dealing with His people. They had faith the promised Seed of David would sit upon the throne of David at Jerusalem, when all nations and peoples would worship together the one true God and universal peace and prosperity would be enjoyed by all.

Anxiously they asked Jesus, "Tell us, when shall these things be? and what shall be the sign of thy coming, and the end of the world." (age) (Mark 13:4) Jesus did not attempt to tell His followers of the devastation coming in the twentieth century; the machine guns and cannons mounted on tanks and battleships, rockets carried on submarines and planes with thunderously explosive atomic bombs. They would be unable to scarcely imagine, but He did give them a few hints of things to come. He also gave them, and us, a few signs of those days, enough for Matthew to record for future generations to study and identify.

Jesus spoke parable after parable describing the nature of the Kingdom of God, but it remained a mystery even to His closest followers. To most people of His day, and even today, the mysteries of the Kingdom of Heaven remain a mystery, and even His disciples puzzled over His explanations.

Our Lord dealt with two main subjects in His discourse, namely; the destruction of Jerusalem and the Second Advent. With regard to each of these, He first mentioned a number of happenings that were not to be taken as 'signs' before giving the important sign that would immediately precede the main event. After Jesus had spoken of events, His disciples were told that these were not to be taken as signs, but only the, "beginnings of sorrows." He then went on to deal with the question, "When shall these things be?"

All three gospel writers record the question, but Mark and Luke add the further question, "What shall be the sign when all these things shall be fulfilled?" From the context in which the question was asked, we know "these signs" to refer to the prophecy concerning the destruction of the Temple. Overlooked by many

Bible scholars is the fact that Christ answered only the first of the two questions. Matt. 24:4, dealt with the destruction of the Temple and the events that were to be expected during the apostolic age. Both were to culminate before the Jewish War and the destruction of Jerusalem in A.D. 70.

Christ particularly emphasized that these preliminary events were nothing to be alarmed about. "Take heed that no man deceive you." (Matt. 24:4) "All these are the beginning of sorrows." (Matt. 24:8) They were not to be taken as signs that the destruction of Jerusalem was imminent. Seemingly, the purpose of these preliminary forecasts was, upon fulfillment, to establish faith in the longer predictions that follow.

A study of the historical events after the Resurrection of Christ will show that this part of the prophecy was fulfilled in every particular before the Jewish War. It is important to establish this in order to refute the widespread error that some of these predictions relate to events at the end of the Christian Era. Such an interpretation throws the whole discourse out of its chronological order.

False Christs

Jesus began His discourse by warning His disciples, "Take heed that no man deceive you. For many shall come in my name, saying, I am Christ; and shall deceive many. (Matt. 24:4-5; Mark 13:5-6) "Take heed that ye be not deceived: for many shall come in my name, saying, I am Christ; and the time draweth near: go ye not therefore after them." (Luke 21:8)

The false Christs were to appear prior to the destruction of Jerusalem and many did make their appearance. Several impostors are mentioned in the Acts of the Apostles. One was Simon, the sorcerer of Samaria who bewitched the people of Samaria, giving out that himself was some great one, "To whom they all gave heed, from the least to the greatest, saying, This man is the great power of God. And to him they had regard, because that of long time he had bewitched them with sorceries." (Acts 8:10-11)

Irenaeus, (Bishop of Lyons, 2nd century A.D.) wrote concerning Simon: "This man was glorified by many as if he were god; and he taught that it was himself who appeared among the Jews as the Son, but descended in Samaria as the Father, while he came to other nations in the character of the Holy Spirit. He represented himself, in a word, as being the loftiest of all powers, that is, the Being who is the Father over all, and he allowed himself to be called by whatsoever title men were please to address him." (Against Heresies, 23, 1) Eusebius informed us that Simon traveled to Rome where he was honored with a statue bearing the inscription, "To Simon the Holy God." (Church Histories 11, 1)

Irenaeus also wrote about a disciple and successor to Simon called Menander, who made similar claims saying he had been sent into the world as a savior for the deliverance of men. His disciples were told they could, "obtain the resurrection of eternal youth." (op.cit. 23, 5) Another impostor was Dositheus who persuaded some of the Samaritans that he was the Christ prophesied by Moses. (Origen Celsius I, 57: VI 2)

In Acts 21:38 we read where Paul was questioned if he was, "that Egyptian, which before these days madest an uproar, and leddest out into the wilderness four thousand men that were murderers?" Josephus relates that the Egyptian in question had marched to the Mount of Olives and threatened Jerusalem, declaring that at his command the walls would fall down. His followers were attacked by Felix and the Roman garrison, though the leader himself escaped. (Antiq. XX, 169. II, 261 ff)

Wars and Rumors of Wars

Jesus next lists troubles or disasters that were to come but not to be taken as "signs." They were events common to all periods of history.

"And ye shall hear of wars and rumours of war; see that ye be not troubled; for all these things must come to pass, but the end is not yet. (Matt. 24:6) "And when ye shall hear of wars and rumours of wars, be ye not troubled: for such things must needs be; but the end shall not be yet." (Mark 13:7) "But when ye shall hear of wars and commotions, be not terrified: for these things must first come to pass; but the end is not by and by." (Luke 21:9)

By the "end" Jesus meant the end of Jerusalem and the Temple about which the disciples had asked. None of the Gospel writers made any mention that Jesus might have referred to the end of the world (age).

Josephus records that following the insurrection of the Egyptian, many other, "religious frauds and bandit chiefs," joined forces and drove numbers to revolt, inciting them to strike a blow for freedom, and threatening with death those who submitted to Roman rule...splitting up into groups, they ranged over the countryside, plundering the houses of the well-to-do, killing the occupants, and setting fire to villages, till their raging madness penetrated every corner of Judea. Day by day the fighting blazed more fiercely." (War. II, 264-266)

Josephus also reported other incidents that almost led to war with Rome. One was the plan to erect a statue of the emperor Galus in the Temple and on another occasion when a Roman soldier was found guilty of indecent exposure in the Temple. (War.

II, 185. Ant. xx 108) These and other events ultimately led to the Jewish War of A.D. 66-70, but until the predicted signs were observed, there was no need to worry.

Nation Shall Rise Against Nation and Kingdom Against Kingdom

In association with the rumors of war Jesus predicted: "For nation shall rise against nation and kingdom against kingdom." (Matt. 24:7; Mark 13:8; Luke 21:10) For many years the Romans were engaged in the conquest of Britain; one battle following another. During the reign of Nero, Rome engaged in a war with Partia over Armenia (Tacitus Ann. Xiii, 4,34) However, it is possible that Jesus was speaking of wars between nations other than the Romans, perhaps involving the Jews. If so, there were many Jewish colonies that experienced hostility in various places. Jews in Babylon were forced to flee to the town of Seleucia peopled by Greeks and Syrians, to escape harassment. Later, when the Babylonians waged all out war on the Jews, the Greeks and the Syrians joined forces with the Babylonians in making war against the Jews, (Ann. XVIII, 374, f.)

Another conflict broke out between the Jews and Syrians in Caesarea, about the time when Paul was imprisoned there by the governor Felix. (Acts 24) The Jews claimed the city was theirs, because it had been built by Herod. The Greeks, although outnumbered by the Jews, had the support of the Roman army, the greater part of which had been recruited in Syria and claimed the city was Greek.

Felix, unable to restore order, referred the matter to Rome. The Syrians, by means of a bribe, obtained an order withdrawing many Jewish privileges. (Antiq. XX, 183; War II, 266) Retaliation by the Jews brought more strife, finally coming to an end in A.D. 66 when the Syrians massacred almost the entire Jewish colony. (War II, 457)

Another example of a war between kingdoms was Rome's conquest of Britain which occupied many years. In the east the kings of Arabia and Parthia were attacking Izates, king of Adiabene on the upper Tigris. There is, therefore, no lack of wars during the apostolic age to which our Lord's prophecy could be applied.

Famines

"And there shall be famines." (Matt. 24:7; Mark 13:8, Luke 21:11) Many times famines occurred in the years that followed Jesus expounding to his disciples what was to come about prior and to the destruction of Jerusalem and the Temple. A widespread famine is recorded in Acts 11:28, "And there stood up one of them named Aqabus, and signified by the spirit that there should be a great dearth throughout all the world: which came to pass in the days of Claudius Caesar." Josephus reported that the famine was particularly severe in Jerusalem where many died for want of food. He also wrote that Queen Helena of Adiabene herself purchased corn from Egypt and dried figs from Cyprus for the inhabitants. Helena's son sent large sums of money for relief work in the city, as did also the Christians in Antioch. (Ant. XX.,51)

Rome itself experienced a severe shortage of food during the reign of Claudius. There was a shortage of corn and when word got out that there was less than fifteen days' supply of food in the city, angry mobs rioted. On one occasion the emperor himself had to be rescued from a hostile crowd by his soldiers. (Tacitus, Ann.XII, 43) Again, during the reign of Nero, there was a shortage of grain in the capital, following a hurricane which had destroyed houses, orchards and crops over a wide area. Hungry mobs foraged the countryside in search of food. (Tacitus Ann. XVL,13)

Pestilences

Pestilences and plagues often followed periods of famine. Tacitus tells that both followed after the ruined harvest, "a plague devastated the entire population of Rome. No miasma was discernible in the air. Yet the houses were full of corpses, and the streets of funerals. Neither sex nor age conferred immunity. Slave or free, all succumbed just as suddenly. Their mourning wives and children were often cremated on the very pyres by which they had sat and lamented." (Tacitus Ann. XVI, 13) According to another account, thirty thousand deaths were actually registered at this time. (Suetonius, Nero, XXXIX) It is possible an even greater number of persons died unrecorded. A pestilence in Babylon at the time the Jews migrated to the city of Seleucia may have been one of the causes of the Jews leaving Babylon.

Earthquakes

"And earthquakes." (Matt. 24:7, Mark 13:8, Luke 21:11) During the apostolic age several earthquakes were severe enough to have been mentioned in history. About A.D. 46, a great earthquake accompanied by a thunderous roar, shook the whole island of Crete. At one place, on the coast, the sea receded nearly a mile, while at the same time a new island rose up out of the sea to the north. (Philostratus, Vit, Apollonius IV, 34) In A.D. 51, the year of the great famine in Rome, there were repeated earthquakes which flattened houses and did widespread damage in the city. (Tacitus Ann., XII, 43)

Two years later, in Asia Minor, an earthquake destroyed the Phrygian city of Apamea. As the result of the catastrophe, the city was granted remission of taxes for five years. (Tacitus Ann., XII, 58) In A.D. 60, another Phrygian city, Laodicea, was devastated by an earthquake whose citizens gained fame by rebuilding the city from their own resources, without the assistance from Rome. (Tacitus Ann., XIV, 27) Then, three years later the town of Pompeii (in Italy) was largely demolished in the same manner. (Tacitus Ann., XV, 22)

In the decade or two preceding the destruction of Jerusalem, the eastern Mediterranean seems to have experienced more earthquakes than any similar period of time in history. Seneca, writing about A.D. 64, remarked, "How often have cities in Asia, how often in Achaic, been laid low by a simple shock of earthquake! How often has Paphos collapsed! Not infrequently are tidings brought to us of utter destruction of entire cities." (Seneca, Epistles, 91, 9) Although these disasters were to be regarded as "portents," Jesus made it clear to His disciples that they had no significance in relationship to the fate of Jerusalem.

Signs in the Heavens

"And fearful sights and great signs shall there be from heaven." (Luke 21:11) In addition to the preliminary events to take place during the apostolic age, recorded by Matthew and Mark, Luke adds another. "But before all these things, they shall lay their hands on you, and persecute you, delivering you up to the synagogues, and into prisons, being brought before kings and rulers for my name's sake." (v.12) It appears that our Lord is saying, the signs from heaven would occur only at the end of the apostolic age, after the trials of the disciples and this is borne out by history.

Josephus tells us, regarding the impending fate of Jerusalem, "First a star stood over the city, very like a broad sword, and a comet that remained a whole year." At another time, in mid-winter before the war began he wrote, "at three in the morning, so bright a light shone around the Altar and the Sanctuary, that it might have been midday. This lasted an hour."

On another occasion before sunset, Josephus reported, "there were seen in the sky over the whole country, chariots and regiments in arms speeding through the clouds and encircling the towns." There must have been some truth in these reports, for similar statements are made by Cornelius Tacitus (Roman historian) in his "histories." Halley's Comet which put in an appearance in the year 68 may have accounted for some of them.

Disciples Experiences

The third set of events that Jesus said would happen, but that were not to be taken as indicating that the destruction of Jerusalem was imminent, dealt with difficulties that the disciples would experience. "Then shall they deliver you up to be afflicted, and shall kill you: and ye shall be hated of all nations for my name's sake. And then shall many be offended, and shall betray one another, and shall hate one another." (Matt. 24:9-10) "But take heed to yourselves: for they shall deliver you up to councils; and in the synagogues ye shall be beaten: and ye shall be brought before rulers and kings for my sake, for a testimony against them." (Mark 13:9) "But before all these, they shall lay their hands on you, and persecute you, delivering you up to the synagogues, and into prisons, being brought before kings and rulers for my name's sake." (Luke 21:12)

At first glance the account recorded in Matthew appears to differ from that of Mark and Luke. However, the reason for this is quite simple. Matthew is known for not always recording events or the teachings of Jesus in their strict chronological order, but usually grouped related subjects together. In this case, the predictions recorded in Mark 13:9-13 and Luke 21:12-19 were more fully recorded by Matthew 10:17-20, along with other instructions that Jesus gave when he commissioned His twelve apostles. Consequently, Matthew gave only a condensed version in chapter 14:9-10. Then, in verses 11-14 he adds some additional material omitted by Mark and Luke in their gospels. It is noteworthy that the predictions given by all three writers were fulfilled before the outbreak of the Jewish Wars in A.D. 66.

Matthew used the Greek word "tote" for "then", meaning at that time. If he had meant "afterwards" he would have used the word "cita." Thus the troubles the disciples were to face at the hands of the officials were to be experienced during the same period as the secular events listed in the previous section, and not at some later date. Luke corroborates this interpretation by his introductory words: "Before all these things they shall lay hands on you, and persecute you."

Official Opposition

The first opposition to the disciples came on the day of Pentecost, when Peter and John healed a lame man at the Beautiful Gate of Jerusalem. The news of this healing spread fast and soon multitudes of sick and ailing people gathered around the disciples. Peter exhorted the people to repentance saying, "the God of Abraham, and of Isaac and of Jacob, the God of our fathers, hath glorified his Son Jesus: whom ye delivered up, and denied him in the presence of Pilate, when he was determined to let him go. But ye denied the Holy One and the Just, and desired a murderer to be granted unto you: And killed the Prince of life, whom God hath raised from the dead; whereof we are witnesses.....Repent ye therefore, and be converted, that your sins may be blotted out, when the times of refreshing shall come from the presence of the Lord." (Acts 3:13-15, 19)

Seeing the response of the people to the words of the disciples, to confess belief in Jesus Christ, the priests and captains of the Temple, "laid hands on them, and put them in hold unto the next day: for it was now eventide." (Acts 4:3) On the next day, Peter and John were brought before an assembly of the "rulers, and elders, and scribes, and Annas, the high priest, and Caiaphas, and John and Alexander, and as many as were of the kindred of the high priest (Sadducees) were gathered together at Jerusalem." (Acts 4:5)

On being questioned by the Temple authorities as to what power they invoked in the healing miracle, Peter answered by testifying against them, saying, "Be it known to you all, and to all the people of Israel, that by the name of Jesus Christ of Nazareth, whom ye crucified, whom God raised from the dead, even by him doth this man stand before you whole." (Acts 4:10) Fearing the wrath of the multitude that had witnessed the miracle, the officials just, "threatened them, they let them go, finding nothing how they might punish them, because of the people: for all men glorified God for that which was done." (Acts 4:21)

Continued witnessing and healing again brought official opposition as the high priest, "and all they that were with him, (which is the sect of the Sadducees,) and were filled with indignation, And laid their hands on the apostles, and put them in the common prison." (Acts 5:17-18) Only on the advice of a Pharisee, named Gamaliel, did the Temple authorities refrain from carrying out their plan to slay Peter and the other disciples.

Not long after this, "Stephen, full of faith and power, did great wonders and miracles among the people. Then there arose certain of the synagogue...And they stirred up the people, and the elders, and the scribes, and caught him and brought him to the council," (Acts 6:9, 12) Stephen also testified against them saying, "Ye stiff necked and uncircumcised in heart and ears, ye do always resist the Holy Ghost: As your fathers did, so do ye." (Acts 7:51) "Then they cried out with a loud voice, and stopped their ears, and ran upon him with one accord...And they stoned Stephen, calling upon God, and saying, Lord Jesus, receive my spirit." (Acts 7:57, 59) Clearly the death of Stephen was fulfillment of Matthew 24:9.

Saul (later called Paul) who consented to the death of Stephen led a great persecution of the young "church" in Jerusalem and with the authority of the priests, "...he made havoc of the church, entering into every house, and haling men and women committed them to prison." (Acts 8:3) Later, Herod, after he had killed James the brother of John with the sword, put Peter in prison, from which he had a miraculous escape. (Acts 12) On another occasion, Paul and Silas, after being severely beaten, were cast into prison at Philippi, where they also had a miraculous escape. (Acts 16:23-40) These persecutions of the disciples were what Jesus had warned His disciples would come upon them, "and some of you shall they cause to be put to death." (Luke 21:16)

Luke recorded Jesus saying that persecution would bring opportunities for "testimony." (Luke 21:13) This prophecy had its perfect fulfillment when Paul was brought before a succession of Roman rulers, beginning with the governor Felix; (Acts 23:24) then his successor Festus and King Agrippa. (Acts 25 and 26) To Felix, Paul witnessed concerning the Christian faith, (Acts 24:24) while to Festus and Agrippa, he related how he had been converted on the road to Damascus, and was now preaching, "That Christ should suffer, and that he should be the first that should rise from the dead, and should shew light unto the people, and to the Gentiles." (nations) (Acts 26:23) Finally, on being sent to Rome to appear before the emperor Caesar, Paul spent two years there, "Preaching the kingdom of God, and teaching those things which concern the Lord Jesus Christ, with all confidence, no man forbidding him." (Acts 28:31)

Divine Guidance

Jesus promised His disciples they would receive Divine guidance in the time of their persecutions. "But when they shall lead you, and deliver you up, take no thought beforehand what ye shall speak, neither do ye premeditate: but whatsoever shall be given you in that hour, that speak ye: for it is not ye that speak, but the Holy Ghost." (Mark 13:11) To Mark's account, Luke adds, "For I will give you a mouth and wisdom, which all your adversaries shall not be able to gainsay nor resist." (Luke 21:15) Matthew reported the same advice, "But when they deliver you up, take no thought how or what ye shall speak: for it shall be given you in that hour what ye shall speak. For it is not ye that speak, but the spirit of your Father which speaketh in you." (Matt. 10:19-20)

Paul's words did confound all opposition to him. When the Roman soldiers that had rescued him from an angry Jewish mob in the Temple and were about to give him a beating themselves, Paul claimed Roman citizenship. He asked, "Is it lawful for you to scourge a man that is a Roman, and uncondemned?" The next day before the Jewish council Paul perceived that his accusers were one part Sadducees and the other part Pharisees. He cried out, "Men and brethren, I am a Pharisee, the son of a Pharisee: of the hope and resurrection of the dead I am called in question." (Acts 23:6) These words immediately threw his accusers into utter confusion, because the Pharisees believe in a resurrection whereas the Sadducees did not.

The Pharisees immediately came to Paul's defense, saying, "We find no evil in this man: but of a spirit or an angel hath spoken to him, Let us not fight against God." (Acts 23:9) Later, when Paul was examined by the Jews before Felix he pointed out that no witness had been brought against him to prove he was guilty of any crimes. At a second hearing before Festus and Agrippa, Paul again claimed Roman citizenship and at the same time maintained his innocence of any wrong doing against the laws of the Jews or the Temple. (Acts 25:8)

Paul's eloquent defense (Acts 26:2-19) was so effective that King Agrippa said, "This man doeth nothing worthy of death or of bonds...This man might have been set at liberty, if he had not appealed unto Caesar." (Acts 26:31-32) In Paul's letter to Timothy telling of his trial in Rome, he wrote; "Notwithstanding the Lord stood with me and strengthened me; that by me the preaching might be fully known, and that all the Gentiles (nations) might hear: and I was delivered out of the mouth of the lion." (II Tim. 4:17)

Persecution

All three Gospels record our Lord's prediction that the disciples as well as the Church would suffer persecution: "..and ye shall be hated of all nations, (Mark 13:13; Luke 2:17) for my sake." (Matt. 24:9) There are those who contend that this prophecy applies to the future, but they fail to explain how this is to happen. While it is true that Christianity is in general hated or persecuted in many parts of the world, in the Christian nations of Western Europe, Scandinavia, British Commonwealth and the United States, this is not so, nor is it likely to be. Even in many non-Christian nations, church missionaries and philanthropic enterprises of Christian churches are welcome.

On the other hand, there is no question but that the early Christians were hated and persecuted from the first by the Jewish authorities, not only in Judea, but in other places, "We are troubled on every side, yet not distressed; we are perplexed, but not in despair; persecuted, but not forsaken; cast down, but not destroyed." (IICor. 4:8-9) Reporting on his missionary journeys, Paul said, "Of the Jews five times received I forty stripes, save one. Thrice was I beaten with rods, one I was stoned." (II Cor. 11:24-25)

While the Christians were at first tolerated by the Romans, following the great fire in Rome (A.D. 64) they suffered their greatest persecutions. Nero put the blame for the fire on, "the notoriously depraved Christians," as Tacitus reported. At first Nero had the self-acknowledged Christians arrested. Then, on their information, acquired by interrogation, large numbers of others were condemned, not necessarily because of the destructive fire, but rather for "anti-social tendencies." (Tacitus, Ann., XV, 44) The pressure, perhaps by threats of torture, on the Christians to betray one another, revealed by Tacitus and other historians, throws light on the prophecy recorded in all three Gospels: "And ye shall be betrayed both by parents, and brethren, and kinsfolks, and friends, and some of you they shall cause to be put to death." (Luke 21:16; Matt. 24:10; Mark 13:12)

False Prophets

A prophecy of Jesus is recorded by Matthew, but omitted by Mark and Luke, says, "And many false prophets shall rise, and shall deceive many." (Matt. 24:11) Since Matthew mentioned "false messiahs" in v. 5 it would appear "false prophets" must refer to a different class of persons; not those claiming to be Christ. One such person may have been Theudas who, in the time of the governor Fasus (about A.D. 45) "persuaded a vast crowd to take their belongings and follow him to the river Jordan; for he claimed to be a prophet and promised to divide the river and provide them with an easy crossing." (Ant., XX, 97) However, it is more probably that the "false prophets" referred to were those in the early church who not only made false predictions, but led many astray by false teachings. The consequences of this are foretold in the next two verses: "And because iniquity (lawlessness) shall abound, the love of many shall wax cold. But he that shall endure to the end, the same shall be saved." (Matt. 24:12-13)

Luke in his version of the discourse reports a warning about false Christs and false prophets, particularly Christians of Judean origin for whom Matthew especially wrote: "Then if any man shall say unto you, Lo, here is Christ, or there; believe it not. For there shall arise false Christs, the false prophets, and shall show great signs and wonders; insomuch that, if it were possible, they shall deceive the very elect. Behold, I have told you before. Wherefore if they shall say unto you, Behold he is in the desert; go not forth. Behold, he is in the secret chambers; believe it not. For as the lightening cometh out of the east, and shineth even unto the west; so that also the coming of the Son of man be." (Matt. 24: 23-27)

Since Matthew had already included a warning about false Christs and false prophets which were to appear before the great tribulation (Matt. 24:5, 11), this further warning can refer only to similar impostors arising after it. This is, of course, incompatible with the notion that the great tribulation is connected with the Second Advent, an event which will be so universally recognizable that no further false Christs could arise.

It is thus implied in Matthew's account that following the great tribulation there would be a period during which there would be false Christs and false prophets. Clearly none of the elect, that is no true Christian, would be deluded by anyone claiming to be the Messiah of Old Testament prophecy, for they knew He had already come. But as to His second coming, we are told that this will be seen throughout the whole world, as lightning shines from east to west. It is in this context that Matthew's version goes on to speak of, "the tribulation of those days."

Paul warned the Galations that, "there be some that trouble you, and would pervert the gospel of Christ." (Gal. 1:7) He also warned Titus that, "There are many unruly and vain talkers and deceivers, especially they of the circumcision, whose mouths must be stopped, who subvert whole houses, teaching things which they ought not." (Titus 1:10-11) In his second letter to Timothy, Paul names two such teachers, "Hymenaeus and Philetue, who concerning the truth have erred, saying that the resurrection is past already and overthrew the faith of some." (II Tim. 2:17-18)

In II Cor. 11:13, Paul speaks of, "false prophets, deceitful workers, transforming themselves into the apostles of Christ." Paul relates that, "Demas hath forsaken me, having loved this present world, and is departed unto Thessalonica...Alexander the coppersmith did me much evil...At my first answer no man stood with me, but all forsook me." (II Tim. 4:10, 14, 16) Paul was actually frightened by the gullibility of the Christians of Corinth. "But I fear, lest by any means, as the serpent beguiled Eve through his subtilty, so your minds should be corrupted from the simplicity that is in Christ. For if he that cometh preacheth another Jesus, whom we have not preached, or if ye receive another spirit, which ye have not received, or another gospel, which ye have not accepted, ye might well bear with him." (II Cor. 11:3-4)

The Gospel Preached

Jesus said; "And this gospel of the kingdom shall be preached in all the world for a witness unto all nations: and then shall the end come." (Matt. 24:4) "And the gospel must be published among all nations." (Mark 13:10) This prophecy of Jesus has been generally misinterpreted to relate to the end of the world. This conclusion is based on two points. First, because Matthew includes in his introduction, the question, "What shall be the sign of thy coming and of the end of the world?" Second, the belief that the gospel was not and could not be preached in all the world until modern times.

With regards to the first point, the Greek word for "end" in verse 14 is not the same as the word "end" in verse 3. The word Matthew used in the disciple's question (ver.3) is "sunteleia" meaning a full and complete end, and is always used with reference to the end of the world. (age) (as in Matt. 13, 39, 40, and 49) The word Jesus used in Matthew 24:13-14 is "telos" and has a completely different meaning. The fact that Jesus did not use the word "sunteleia" makes it very clear that He was not answering the second part of the disciple's question.

Obviously the "end" (telos) referred to the end of the Temple in Jerusalem, the central theme of Jesus' prophecy. Most scholars accept the same word, "telos" used in Matthew 24:6 ("the end-telos-is not yet") refers to the Temple. The answer to the question in verse 3, regarding the end of the world, is given later in its proper context in verse 29 and 30, where it is the same as that given in Mark 13:24-25 and Luke 21:25-26.

The second point can only be upheld if the expression, "in all the world" is interpreted in a manner different from its usage elsewhere in the New Testament. For example, it has never been supposed that when Caesar Augustus made a decree, "that all the world should be taxed," (Luke 2:1) that he included Australia, Japan and the Americas. Nor is there evidence that the "great dearth throughout all the world" predicted by Agabus (Acts 11:28) which occurred in the days of Claudius Caesar, was worldwide. In fact, within the correct meaning of the term used in the New Testament, the gospel was preached, "in all the world," before the destruction of Jerusalem and the Temple in A.D. 70, as Jesus predicted and authenticated by Biblical history.

Paul, writing to the Roman church, thanks God that their faith, "is spoken throughout the whole world," (Rom. 1:8) and he told the Colossians that, "the gospel which ye have heard was preached to every creature which is under heaven." (Col. 1:23) Obviously Paul's words were metaphoric in meaning. Eusebius, in his History of the Church, recorded that, "in accordance with the Holy Scriptures, the voice of its inspired evangelists and apostles went forth into all the earth, and their words to the end of the world. In every town and village, like a well-filled threshing floor, churches shot up bursting with eager members." (II,3.) Eusebius gave more particulars, "The holy apostles and disciples of our Saviour were scattered over all the world. Thomas, tradition tells us, was chosen for Parthia, Andrew for Scythia, John for Asia, where he remained till his death in Ephesus." (III, 1) He also tells us that at the end of the second century a missionary was sent to India, and, "found that Matthew's gospel had arrived before him, and was in the hands of some there who had come to know Christ. Bartholomew, one of the apostles, had preached to them and had left behind Matthew's account written in Aramaic character." (v.10)

At the other end of the world, (figuratively speaking) we learn from the British historian Gildas Badonicus, (A.A. 516-570) that the British Isles received the precepts of Christ, "in the latter part of the reign of Tiberius Caesar, by whom his religion was propagated without impediment." (Gildas 8) Thus, Gildas,

Eusebuis and the Scriptures themselves, witness to the fact that the gospel was, "preached in all the world for a witness."

We have now covered the first part of the Olivet Prophecies as recorded by Matthew 24, up to verse 35; Mark 13, up to verse 23, and Luke 21 up to verse 24, and have seen that everything predicted was fulfilled before the Jewish War that began in A.D. 66. There was nothing special or peculiar about the events which could happen at any time. The disciples were distinctly told that they were notto be taken as signs. Neither wars, famines, pestilences, nor earthquakes have any more significance as portents than the persecution of Christians who propagated the gospel. In the next section we shall go on to consider those signs that were to be significant.

The Abomination of Desolation

In the first part of His discourse Jesus had spoken about many things that His disciples were not to regard as signs; "All these are the beginning of sorrows," He said. Following this He went on to deal with the main question He had been asked, "Tell us, when shall these things be?" (Matt. 24:3; Mark 13:4) "Master, but when shall these things be: and what sign will there be when these things shall come to pass?" (Luke 21:4)

In Matthew 24:15-16 and Mark 13:14, the sign given is the abomination of desolation: "When ye therefore shall see the abomination of desolation, spoken of by Daniel the prophet, stand in the holy place, (whoso readeth, let him understand:) Then let them which be in Judea flee into the mountains." "But when ye shall see the abomination of desolation, spoken of by Daniel the prophet, standing where it ought not, (let him that readeth understand) then let them that be in Judea flee to the mountains:" Luke's version (21:20-21) reads, "And when ye shall see Jerusalem compassed with armies then know that the desolation thereof is nigh. Then let them which are in Judea flee to the mountains; and let them which are in the midst of it depart out; and let not them that are in the countries enter therein."

It has been widely supposed that the abomination of desolation means the Roman armies which besieged Jerusalem in A.D. 70. But the Roman armies encircling the city outside the walls cannot be the same thing as an abomination standing in the holy place inside the city. Another explanation has been given that after the fall of Jerusalem, the Romans brought their standards into the Temple and offered sacrifices to them there. (War VI, 316)

But if the abomination standing in the holy place is to be understood as the Roman army offering sacrifices in the Temple after Jerusalem had fallen, how could anyone take this as a sign that those in Judea should flee to the mountains? By that time all the worst features of the war and ensuing siege were over. To be any value as a sign, the abomination of desolation must have appeared in the holy place early enough for the people to get out and flee to the mountains before the siege began.

The abomination of desolation was actually a double sign given to the inhabitants of Jerusalem. The first would be obvious when Jerusalem was encompassed by armies. The second was reference to the abomination spoken of by Daniel the prophet which all those cognizant of the writings of Daniel would understand. Jesus added the comment, "Whoso readeth let him understand." This suggests that before reading this prophecy, it is necessary to understand what Daniel had to say on the matter.

Daniel makes mention of the abomination in chapter 9. This prophecy, known as, "The Seventy Weeks," foretells the coming of Christ to atone for sin and redeem His people within a given period, said to be seventy weeks, and then briefly outlines the subsequent fate of Jerusalem. Here we find the significant prediction that, "the people of the prince that shall come shall destroy the city and the sanctuary." (v. 26), clearly an allusion to the destruction of Jerusalem and the Temple, the very subject about which the disciples had asked.

The prophecy adds, in the final verse, that, "for the overspreading of abominations he shall make it desolate, even until the consummation," which means till the end of the age. Whatever may be the precise meaning of the intervening words, there appears to be here a prediction of abominations on account of which Jerusalem and the sanctuary were to be made desolate until the end of the Christian era. It appears from this prophecy that these abominations were to occur immediately before Jerusalem was destroyed and made desolate in A.D. 71, and for this reason they would clearly be a suitable sign of that event.

In this prophecy, to which particular reference is evidently made in both Matthew's and Mark's version of our Lord's discourse, Daniel was told that within a period of seventy weeks of Hebrew history, six features of the Atonement listed in verse 24 of Daniel's prophecy would be accomplished. "Seventy weeks are determined upon thy people and upon the holy city, to finish the transgression, and to make an end of sins, and to make reconciliation for iniquity, and to bring in everlasting righteousness, and to seal up the vision and the prophecy, and to anoint the most Holy."

A further prophecy about the abomination of desolation is to be found in Daniel 11:31, "And arms shall stand on his part, and they shall pollute the sanctuary of strength, and shall take away the daily sacrifice." This verse follows a passage in Daniel, (11:21-30) in which the career of Antiochus Epiphanes, king of Syria, (173-164 B.C.) had been foretold. In that section, the pronoun "he" refers throughout to Antiochus, but in verse 31 the pronoun is "they" which refers to the arms, or armies, that take his part or place. Most Bible readers fail to notice the change from he to they, and so imagine that verses 31 to 35 continue to refer to the affairs of Antiochus Epiphanes. But when the facts of history are carefully compared, it will be found that they do not agree with the terms of the prophecy in verses 31 to 35, although it is often thought that they do.

Our knowledge of this king comes mainly from the Books of the Maccabees, where we learn that in 167 B.C. Antiochus Epiphanes sent an army of 22,000 men who plundered Jerusalem: "The king sent to the towns of Judea a high revenue official, who arrived at Jerusalem with a powerful force. His language was friendly, but full of guile. For once he had gained the city's confidence, he suddenly attacked it. He dealt it a heavy blow, and killed many Israelites, plundering the city and setting it ablaze." (I Macc. 1:29-31; 2 Macc. 5:24) His army is also said to have defiled the holy place (v.37), but nowhere is it said that they set up an abomination of desolation.

Later Antiochus issued a decree that all his subjects must change their religion, and he sent his agents who, with the aid of some renegade Jews, polluted the sanctuary and set up a pagan altar: "The king sent agents with written orders to Jerusalem and the towns of Judaea. Ways and customs foreign to the country were to be introduced. Burnt offerings, sacrifices and libations in the temple wereforbidden; sabbaths and feastdays were to be profaned; the temple and its ministers to be defiled. Altars, idols and sacred precincts were to be established; swine and other unclean beasts to be offered in sacrifice....He appointed superintendents over all the people, and instructed the towns of Judaea to offer sacrifice town by town....On the fifteenth day of the month Kislev in the year 167 B.C., 'the abomination of desolation' was set up on the altar. Pagan altars were built throughout the towns of Judaea....On the twenty-fifth day of the month they offered sacrifice on the pagan altar which was on top of the altar of the Lord." (1 Macc. 1:44-59; cf. 2 Macc. 6:1-2)

Here the pagan altar is said to be the abomination of desolation but this must be a false application of Daniel's prophecy, for according to our Lord's discourse the abomination of desolation was still future in A.D. 33. Furthermore, no army was involved which Daniel 11:31 requires, neither can the circumstances in any way be related to Daniel's prophecy in chapter 9, which says the sanctuary would thereafter remain desolate till the end of the age.

After the time of Antiochus Epiphanes, Roman armies had invaded the holy precincts on four separate occasions (Antiq. XIV, 66; XIV, 105; XIV, 482; War II, 47) but far from being made desolate, the Temple had since been entirely rebuilt by Herod the Great, and was, in the time of Christ, more glorious than at any time since the days of Solomon. Herod the Great who desired to kill the Child Jesus of Bethlehem (Matt. 2:16) had unknowingly prepared the Temple to receive the Lord Jesus Christ. The "glory of this latter house" did become "greater than the former" as the latter was hallowed by the presence of Christ as the prophet Haggai had foretold to Zerubbabel. (Haggai 2:9)

Consequently the Jews seem to have realized that Daniel's prophecy would not be fulfilled by foreign armies, but was to have its fulfillment when Jewish armies would pollute the house of God. Thus, Josephus says that, "there was an age-old saying of inspired men, that the city would be taken and the most Holy Temple burnt to the ground by right of war, if ever the citizens strove with each other, and Jewish hands were the first to pollute the house of God." (War. IV, 388)

No Old Testament prophecy says precisely this, but it could be an inference drawn from Daniel 11:31 in view of the fact that, although the Romans had several times polluted the sanctuary, the Temple had not been destroyed. When we turn to examine the events of the Jewish War of A.D. 66-70 we shall see that they confirm this view. This war began when the Jews, incensed by the iniquitous rule of the Roman procurator Florus, had revolted.

Josephus tells us that, "Eleazar, son of Ananias the high priest, and a very competent and young man, who was Temple captain, persuaded the ministers of the Temple to accept no gift or offering from a foreigner. This is what made the war inevitable; for they abolished the sacrifices offered for Rome and Caesar." (War II, 409)

When Eleazar and his followers took possession of the Temple in Jerusalem, he was opposed by the leading citizens, the chief priests, and others desiring peace with Rome who occupied the western and southern parts of the city. Fighting soon broke out between these two factions, and mutual slaughter continued for seven days, while the Roman garrison was powerless to keep order. In his account of these events. Josephus speaks of Eleazar and the insurgents "polluting the sanctuary." (War. II, 423)

Josephus then records that shortly afterwards, the insurgents burnt down the house of Ananias the high priest, who then took refuge in the sewers, only to be caught the next day and murdered. (War. II, 426,441) Following this incident, another body of revolutionaries arrived in Jerusalem from Massada, which they had captured from the Romans. Eleazar could not tolerate a rival, so he and his men attacked and massacred the newcomers in the Temple. (War. II, 434-448)

Shortly after the massacre the Roman garrison surrendered on the condition that their lives would be spared. The revolutionaries agreed to this, but as soon as the Romans laid down their arms, Eleazar and his men slaughtered them. (War. II, 450) This murderous army of insurgents, who called themselves Zealots, continued to occupy and pollute the sanctuary throughout the whole war, from the summer of 66 until the city was captured and destroyed by the Romans in A.D. 70. They fulfilled the prophecies concerning the abomination of desolation.

In consequence of the Jewish Revolt, the Roman general Cestius mustered his forces in Syria and marched on Jerusalem, where a large number of Jews had gathered to celebrate the Feast of Tabernacles in Oct. 66. When he pitched his camp on Mount Scopus, less than a mile from Jerusalem, the insurgents retreated to the inner city and the strongly fortified temple area, while the priests and leading citizens tried to sue for peace.

The Romans, however, kept up their attacks from all sides for several days and began to assault the Temple itself. Then for no apparent reason Cestius suddenly called his men back and retired from the siege. The revolutionary Jews at once took advantage of this and sallying forth, very soon turned the Roman withdrawal into an ignominious defeat. (War. II, 513-555)

Thus in the autumn of A.D. 66, it came about that both the signs given by Jesus to herald the destruction of the Temple were seen to be fulfilled. The holy place was being polluted by the abominations done by the Jewish revolutionary army, while outside the walls the Roman armies had encompassed Jerusalem. The Christian community was not slow to notice this. Eusebius tells us that, "The members of the Jerusalem church, by means of an oracle given by revelation to acceptable persons there, were ordered to leave the city before the war began, and settle in a town in Peraea, called Pella. To Pella, those who believed in Christ migrated from Jerusalem." (Church History III, 5)

Josephus likewise, without acknowledging that it was mainly the Christian community who were involved, records that, "After the disastrous defeat of Cestius' army, many prominent Jews fled from the city like swimmers from a sinking ship." (War. II, 556) It is a great pity that many church leaders today mislead people into believing that the abomination of desolation is some future phenomenon, and fail to realize that what was so obvious to those who saw it at the time, namely that it was already manifest in the holy place in A.D. 66.

The Assault On Jerusalem

Following the unsuccessful siege of Jerusalem by Cestius and the route of his army at the end of Oct., both Jews and Romans prepared for a full scale war. At a mass meeting in the Temple, the Jews, including those who had hitherto favored peace with Rome, appointed generals to take charge in various parts of the country. (War. II, 562-568) Among those was Josephus who later wrote a history of the war. He was given command of Galilee, but soon independent gangs of robbers sprang up in the same province. One of those waylayed the chief minister of King Agrippa and robbed him of all his baggage as well as a large amount of money. (War. II, 595) Another group four hundred strong led by John of Gischala was plundering all Galilee. (War. II, 585)

According to Matthew's and Mark's account, our Lord emphasized the need for taking speedy action when the abominations were seen in the Temple: "Let him which is on the housetop not come down to take anything out of his house: neither let him which is in the field return back to take his clothes. And woe unto them that are with child, and to them that give suck in those days; But pray ye that your flight be not in winter, neither on the sabbath day." (Matt. 24:17-20)

The significance of these words will be appreciated when it is realized that the defeat of Cestius occurred at the end of October. Already daylight hours, to which traveling was limited in those days, were getting shorter, while winter with its rainy season was fast approaching. Also, owing to the danger from gangs of bandits, speed was all important and those with children would not be able to travel fast. Traveling on the sabbath day was severely limited by

Jewish law. There can be little doubt that our Lord's warnings and advice were particularly suited to the situation and circumstances immediately after the defeat of Cestius in the late autumn of A.D. 66. By the following spring the whole country was overrun by gangs of bandits, and fresh Roman armies were arriving in an attempt to suppress the revolt. The brief interval before the winter was practically the last opportunity for anyone to escape from Jerusalem. A short survey of the course of the war from A.D. 66 to 70 will confirm this, and shed light on the mounting scale of abominations perpetrated by the Jews in the Temple. Following the defeat of Cestius, the Emperor Nero in Rome called on his most experienced general, Vespasian, a veteran of campaigns in Germany and Britain, to take charge of affairs in Palestine. While Vespasian assembled the Roman forces from the north in Syria, his son Titus sailed to Egypt to collect another army from there. (War. III, 29, 64) Together they launched an attack on Galilee, a campaign which occupied the greater part of the year 67.

Josephus, after being besieged in Jotapata, finally surrendered. (War. III, 132-408) But John of Gischala and many of his followers fled from Galilee to Jerusalem which they regarded as an impregnable fortress. (War. IV, 106)

Meanwhile in the south, Simon, son of Gioras, collected a band of insurgents who ravaged the countryside and looted the houses of the rich. When the rulers in Jerusalem tried to curb his activities, Simon retired into the stronghold of Masada from where he continued to launch his raids. (War. II, 653) Vespasian, after subduing Galilee, marched south along the coastal plain but he was not the only menace to the Jews.

The Jewish Civil War

Josephus reported, "Every town was seething with turmoil and civil war, and as soon as the Romans gave them a breathing space, they turned their hands against each other. Between advocates of war and lovers of peace, there was a fierce quarrel. First of all in the home, finally unity was disrupted by partisan bitterness; then the nearest kinsmen severed all ties of blood, and attaching themselves to men who thought as they did, lined up on opposite sides...They began by one and all plundering their neighbors, then forming themselves into companies, they extended their organized robbery of the countryside...When at last the leaders of the various gangs of bandits had had enough of plundering the countryside, they came together and formed a single pack of rogues. Then they infiltrated into Jerusalem, a city without military command, where by age-old custom any of Jewish race were admitted without scrutiny." (War. IV, 131-135)

Sounds like Edomite "Jews" against Judahites

Josephus goes on to record that, not content with theft and brigandage, these bandits next took to murdering rich and prominent people in Jerusalem. "Terror filled the people, and as if the city had been taken by storm, no one thought of anything but his own safety." (War. IV, 142) Finally the terrorists got control of the appointment of chief priests, setting aside the families which traditionally provided these. Obscure people who thus found themselves in high office were inevitably the tools of those who put them there, and became partners in their crimes. (War. IV, 147-149) *Same as what happend in Northern Kingdom*

One of the rabble of the city was appointed to the priesthood by lot, was robed in the sacred vestments and amid shouts of laughter, was made to carry out the duties of the priestly office.

(War. IV, 155-157) This was so offensive to the populace, they called a mass meeting which was addressed by the chief priest Anaus, "How wonderful it would have been," he declared, "if I had died before seeing the house of God full of countless abominations, and its unapproachable sacred precincts crowded with those whose hands are red with blood." (War. IV, 163)

On hearing about this meeting, the Zealots charged out of the Temple, and a battle ensued in which stones and spears were flung. "The slaughter on both sides was frightful," says Josephus, "and the wounded could no be counted. Casualties on the people's side were carried into the houses by relatives; if a Zealot was hit he went into the Temple, leaving bloodstains on the sacred floor. It might indeed be said that their blood alone polluted the Sanctuary.

After this the Zealots became besieged in the Temple which was, however, well stocked with food. But fearing that the citizens might call on the Romans for help, they sent for assistance from the Idumeans. (War. IV, 228) They managed to get a letter through to them, and soon a sizable Idumean army appeared before the walls of Jerusalem...At first the citizens barred the gates against them, but one night during a storm, some Zealots crept out of the Temple and opened the gates. Another ferocious battle followed, and by morning corpses lay everywhere. (War. IV, 313) "The entire outer Temple was deluged with blood," says Josephus.

After plundering the city and murdering the chief priests, "The Zealots and a solid mass of Idumeans fell upon the population and butchered them like a herd of unclean animals. (War. IV 326) Soon, however, the Idumeans became tired by the senseless slaughter and no material gain by them, went home, but the Jewish Zealots became more arrogant than ever. Some of the people tried to escape their clutches by leaving Jerusalem, "but flight was difficult as every exit was guarded and anyone going out, whatever the reason, was assumed to be on his way to the Romans, and dispatched forthwith...Dead bodies along all the main roads were heaped high, and many who were anxious to desert decided instead to perish in Jerusalem. (War. IV, 378-380)

In addition to the Zealots in the capital, all parts of Judaea continued to be overrun by gangs of bandits who plundered one village after another with impunity. (War. IV, 406-409) Meanwhile the Roman army held aloof, Vespasian, regarding these internal division as a godsend, thinking that any intervention would only serve to reunite the enemy. (War. IV, 386-389) Such was the situation when the emperor, Nero, met a violent death in June, 68. (War. IV, 491)

Nero was succeeded by Vespasian, who left his son Titus to continue the war in Palestine, all of which delayed the Roman attack on Jerusalem. During the lull, Simon, son of Gioras, who had earlier taken refuge in Masada, fathered a revolutionary army with which he first gained control of southern Judaea. Alarmed at this rival faction, the Zealots marched out from Jerusalem against him, but they were defeated and driven back into the city. (War. IV, 514)

Then in the spring of A.D. 59, Simon advanced on Jerusalem where the citizens were living in fear of John of Gischala, who had come from Galilee and became leader of the Zealots. In order to overthrow John, the people allowed Simon and his army to enter, and once again the Zealots were besieged in the Temple. (War. IV, 466-467) Later, however, the Zealot party split in two.

Eleazar, their original leader, could not tolerate being under John who had come later on the scene, so he barricaded himself and his followers in the Inner Temple, while John was confined to the outer court. The rest of the city was controlled by Simon and his army from the south. Fierce fighting between these three factions continued right up till the Roman army, under Titus, began the final siege early in the year A.D. 70. (War. V, 1-39)

John was assailed from both sides but to whatever part of the city he turned to, when he was forced to retreat, he never failed to set fire to the houses that were stocked with grain and supplies of every kind. As he withdrew, Simon advanced and followed his example. It was as if to oblige the Romans they were destroying all that the city had laid up against a siege and sabotaging their defense. The result was that all the buildings round the Temple were burnt to the ground.

The city became a desolate no-man's land where they slaughtered each other and destroyed almost all the grain, that could have supported them through several years of siege. It was hunger that defeated the city, a thing that might never have happened if they had not brought it on themselves. "The entire city was the battleground for these plotters and their disreputable followers, and between them the people were being torn to bits like a great carcase. Old men and women, overwhelmed by the miseries within, prayed for the Romans to come, and looked forward to the war without, which would free them from the miseries within." (War. V, 27)

When the Romans arrived, the rival factions joined forces for a brief period to sally forth against them, but they were soon driven back within the walls of the city, and old rivals resumed their battles. At the Feast of the Passover, however, Eleazar's men allowed worshipers to enter the Inner Temple. John managed to smuggle in among them a gang of armed men, and another fierce fight ensued between the two Zealot factions. (War. V, 98-105) These Zealots continued to occupy the Temple area in opposition to Simon, who controlled the remainder of the city.

Three things are predicted in Daniel 11:31 concerning the armies which took possession of Palestine after Antiochus Epiphanes: "They shall pollute the sanctuary of strength, and shall take away the daily sacrifice, and they shall place the abomination that maketh desolate." It is obvious that the Zealot army that occupied the Temple from the beginning of the war, certainly polluted the sanctuary, and the abominations that they perpetrated were such as to lead to the vengeance of God being poured out on Jerusalem by the Romans.

Following the Passover, in the spring of A.D. 70, the two factions inside the Temple joined forces and even after the Romans had encamped outside the walls, they continued to harass and plunder the populace in the outer parts of the city. Since most of the corn and grain had been destroyed, "men broke into the houses and ransacked them. If they found some, they maltreated the occupants for saying there was none; if they did not, they suspected them of having hidden it more carefully and tortured them...While the strong had more than enough, the weak were in desperate straits...Torments horrible even to hear about, they inflicted on people to make them admit possession of one loaf, or reveal the hiding place of a single handful of barley." (War V, 425, 435)

Josephus tells us, "As the famine became more intense, it devoured whole houses and families. The roofs were covered with women and babes too weak to stand, the streets full of old men already dead – Young men and boys, swollen with hunger, haunted the squares like ghosts, and fell wherever faintness overtook them. To bury their kinsfolk was beyond the strength of the sick, and those who were fit, shirked the task because of the number of the dead and uncertainty about their own fate; for many, while burying others, fell dead themselves." (War. V, 512f.)

Josephus goes on to relate how one woman who had been robbed of her food, laid hands on her own child, "killed him, then roasted him and ate one half, concealing and saving up the rest. At once the partisans appeared and sniffing unholy smell, threatened that if she did not produce what she had prepared, they would kill her on the spot. She replied that she had kept a fine helping for them, and uncovered what was left of her child." (War. VI, 201-212) But they were so overcome with horror that they found themselves unable to accept her invitation.

In these events we can see the curse of God, proclaimed in Leviticus 26: "And ye shall eat the flesh of your sons. and the flesh of your daughters shall ye eat. And I will destroy your high places, and cut down your images, and cast your carcases upon the carcases of your idols, and my soul shall abhor you." (v. 29-30) This was another of those, "things which are written," being fulfilled. In fact, our Lord may have been alluding to such an incident when He continued, "But woe unto them that are with child and to them that give suck in those days! for there shall be great distress in the land, and wrath upon this people." (Luke 21:23)

After the fierce hostility that had been generated by the citizens when they had set aside the qualified priesthood, the Zealots did not dare to interfere with the continued offering of the daily sacrifices. Nevertheless, when the Romans broke through the northern defenses of Jerusalem, later in A.D. 70, and captured the fortress of Antonia at the northeast corner of the Temple Area, Josephus tells us that on the 17th of Panemos (Tammuz), through a lack of men, the Continual Sacrifice had been discontinued, and that the people were in consequence in the depths of despair. (War. VI, 94)

Thus, it was not the Romans, but the army of Zealots occupying the Temple who brought the daily sacrifices to an end some time before the city finally fell, thus fulfilling the third remaining item of the prophecy of Daniel 11:31. As we can see, the events that took place in the time of Antiochus Epiphanes did not agree with the terms of the prophecy, but in A.D. 70 every detail was fulfilled exactly.

To summarize Daniel's predictions, we can see that the abomination of desolation is a term that can only be understood by references to the prophecies of Daniel, in particular that in Daniel 9:27, which says that, "for the overspreading of abominations he shall make it desolate, even until the consummation." These abominations were perpetrated by the Zealots occupying the Temple from A.D. 66 to 70, on account of which God, acting through the agency of the Roman army, made Jerusalem desolate. It is evident, therefore, that the term Abomination of Desolation cannot be applied to anything that is to occur at the end of the age.

The Populace of Jerusalem

Josephus gives us an interesting insight into the makeup of the populace of Jerusalem during this period. It consisted of a racially mixed people consisting in part of Babylonian, Hittite and Edomite origins. He records the early history of the Edomites and how Isaac's son Esau left the land of his father and dwelt among the Horites known later as Edomites or Idumeans (as called by the Greeks). When the Judeans were taken captive to Babylon, the Edomites moved into the vacated Judean lands including Jerusalem. Some seventy years later when the Judeans were allowed to return to their homeland, their arrival triggered conflict with the Edomites.

At first, the two sides plagued each other with raids, but ultimately the returning Judeans became strong enough to become the dominate force in Palestine. The complete subjection of the Edomites by the Judeans came about when John Hycanus (135-105 B.C.) crushed all Edomite resistance and forced them to integrate into not only the "Jewish" (originally meaning remnant of Judah) state, but also into the Jewish religion. This included those in the outlying districts in addition to Jerusalem.

"Hyrcanus took also Dora and Marissa, cities of Idumea, subdued all the Idumeans; and...they submitted to the use of circumcision, and the rest of the Jewish ways of living; at which time therefore they befall them that they were hereafter no other than Jews." (Book XIII, ch. IX Sec. 1)

Although the merger of the Edomites into the Israelite nation was the end of the Edomites as a distinct people in Palestine, their influence was to plague the Judeans and eventually bring about the downfall of the House of Judah. The new Idumean 'converts,' now a legalized part of the Jewish nation, began to seize power by any means at their disposal. The House of Hyrcanus itself, was finally deposed by the Idumean councilor Antipater, who called in the help of the Nabataeans. The Edomite Idumeans remained in power in Hebrew life throughout the time of Christ.

It was an Idumean, Herod I, who upon gaining authority, ordered the extermination of the Hasmonaean priestly line from which Josephus, himself, claimed descent. This same Herod ordered the massacre of the infants when Jesus Christ was born. Herod's son, (Herod the Tetrarch) being the son of an Idumean father and his Samaritan wife, perhaps without a single drop of Israelite blood in his veins, was responsible for the murder of John the Baptist.

It is only logical that the Edomites, as descendants of Esau, would resent the loss to Israel of what once appeared to be their birthright and aspire dominion for themselves, which could only be gained at the expense of the religion of Israel. The Israelite Jews clung tenaciously to all that was Hebrew and it was they who opposed the acceptance of Hellenism into the mainstream of their Hebrew religion. The Idumean Jews on the other hand, embraced it and sought to substitute it for the true Hebrew religion.

In the light of Josephus' history of the Jews concerning the Edomites, it is not unreasonable to assume they were instrumental in flaming the hatreds of the populace that resulted in the abominations, plundering and murdering that took place during the Jewish Wars. During the time of Christ the term "Jew" was used to identify anyone and everyone living in Judea of any nationality or ethnic background. Eventually, people of every race who became proselytes to Judaism called themselves "Jew." The word "Judaism" itself, has come to have more than one meaning. Early Christianity defines it as coming from the Old Testament Hebrewism whereas modern Jewry holds that, "Judaism was not evolved in Judah; it was in Babylon that Judaism first became that which it was and still is." (Harmsworth's History of the Jews, written by Dr. H. Winckle, L.M. King, Dr. R.G. Brandis and H.R. Hall - Vol. 3, pages 1781-4)

Professor H. Graetz, in his long History of the Jews, (Vol. II, Pg. 631, published 1893) says of the Jewish Talmud, "The Babylonian Talmud is especially distinguished from the Jerusalem or Palestine Talmud...it was for this reason that the Babylonian rather than the Jerusalem Talmud became the fundamental possession of the Jewish Race, its life breath, its very soul." Thus eminent Jewish scholars inform us that Judaism, rather than being the religion of ancient Israel is the religion of ancient Babylon.

Josephus also tells us that the returning Judeans from Babylon brought with them to Jerusalem many Babylonian customs and religion, which explains why Jesus criticized some of the priesthood in Jerusalem as following tradition instead of the laws of Moses. The word "Jew," like "Judean," also has more than one meaning. "Behold, I will make them of the synagogue of Satan, which say they are Jews, and are not, but do lie; behold I will make them to come and worship before thy feet, and to know that I have loved thee." (Rev. 3:9)

The Great Tribulation

After answering the disciple's questions about the destruction of the Temple and describing various happenings that were not to be taken as signs to be alarmed about, Jesus then came to the really significant sign, the abomination that would lead to the desolation of Jerusalem and the Temple. The point that Jesus wished to emphasize was that immediately the sign was recognized, urgent measures were to be taken, because the great tribulation would follow in a very short time, "For," he continued, "then shall be great tribulation, such as was not since the beginning of the world to this time, no, nor ever shall be. And except those days should be shortened, there should no flesh be saved; but for the elect's sake those days shall be shortened." (Matt. 24:21-22) Mark's version conveys the same meaning: "For in those days shall be affliction, such as was not from the beginning of the creation which God created unto this time, neither shall be. And except that the Lord had shortened those days, no flesh should be saved: but for the elect's sake, whom He hath chosen, he hath shortened the days. (Mark 13:19-20) "For these days of vengeance, that all things which are written may be fulfilled...And they shall be led away captive into all the nations: and Jerusalem shall be trodden down of the Gentiles, until the times of the Gentiles be fulfilled." (Luke 21:22,24) Since all three gospels are reporting the same discourse, where Luke speaks of "great distress in the land," this must be the great tribulation in the parallel verses in Matthew and Mark. Then when we compare the historical records of the Jewish Wars with the details of the prophecy, there should be no doubt but that the great tribulation occurred in A.D. 70, and in particular that this tribulation was really, "such as was not since the beginning of the world to this time."

Preterism   –59–

We cannot foresee what tribulations may occur in the future, other than to note the tribulation foretold by Daniel 12:1 at the time of the end. "And at that time shall Michael stand up, the great prince which standeth for the children of thy people: and there shall be a time of trouble, such as never was since there was a nation even to that same time: and at that time thy people shall be delivered, every one that shall be found written in the book."

Because Luke's account of the great tribulation quotes Jesus as saying, "For these be the days of vengeance, that all things which are written may be fulfilled." (21:22), some ministers preach today that God has postponed all vengeance until the future day of judgment. They point out that Luke 4:18-19, when recording Jesus reading from the Book of Isaiah chapter 61, declared, "The Spirit of the Lord is upon me, because he hath anointed me to preach good tidings unto the meek; He hath sent me to bind up the brokenhearted, to proclaim liberty to the captives, and the opening of the prison to them that are bound. To proclaim the acceptable year of the Lord. Then He stopped, but had He continued, He would have read, "and the day of vengeance of our Lord."

However, Jesus, shortly before His discourse on the Mount of Olives, had accused the Pharisees of being guilty as their fathers in killing the prophets and asked, "How can ye escape the damnation of Hell." (Matt. 23:33) But retribution was not to wait until the final day of judgment and vengeance fell upon that generation in A.D. 70.

Josephus, in his history of the Jewish War, repeatedly confirms that the curse of God had fallen on Jerusalem and the Jews. Regarding the blood-bath that followed the deposition of the hereditary priests by the Zealots, he declared, "I think God had sentenced this polluted city to destruction, and willed that the Sanctuary should be purged with fire." (War. IV, 323) Again, regarding the siege of Jerusalem, he wrote, "It was God who condemned the whole nation and turned every means of escape to their destruction. (War. V, 559)

Josephus even quotes Titus, the Roman commander, as attributing his success to God: "Faction, hunger, siege, walls that fall when no engine is at work- what else can be the cause but God's anger with them and aid to ourselves." (War. VI, 40) He not only believed that the curse of God had fallen upon Jerusalem, but he seems to have been aware that prophecy, possibly that of Daniel 11:31 was being fulfilled.

Following the suspension of the daily sacrifice, Titus made a final appeal to the people of Jerusalem to surrender, and asked, "Who doesn't know the writings of the old prophets, and the oracle pronounced against this unhappy city and now about to be fulfilled? They foretold the day of her fall - the day when some man began the slaughter of his fellow-countrymen. And aren't the city and Temple full of your dead bodies? It is God, then, God Himself who is bringing with the Romans fire to purge the Temple and is blotting out the city brimful of corruption, as if it had never been." (War. VI, 109) This is exactly what our Lord meant, when He declared, "These be the days of vengeance, that all things which are written may be fulfilled." (Luke 21:22)

Equally significant is the testimony of Josephus to the severity of this time of trouble which he declared to be "the greatest of all time." (War. I, 4) He went on to say that, "the misfortunes of all other races since the beginning of history, compared to those of the Jews, seem small; and for our misfortunes we have only ourselves to blame. (War. V, 442) Again he says, "No other city has ever endured such horrors, and no generation in history has fathered such wickedness." (War. V, 442) In Another place he says, "No destruction ever wrought by God or man approached the wholesale carnage of this war." (War. VI, 428)

These are unsolicited testimonies of a Jew (Judean) and a descendant of the Hasmoneans, who was an eye-witness to the mutual extermination by famine and torture which the Jews brought upon themselves.

Shortening of the Day

Our Lord in His prophecy said that, "Except those days should be shortened, there should no flesh be saved: but for the elect's sake those days shall be shortened." (Matt. 24:22) By the elect, Jesus probably meant a small remnant of Christians who had remained behind in Jerusalem, having for some reason been unable to take flight before the siege began. The word elect usually denoted Christian believers, as it does in verse 24 that follows. But as regards the shortening of the days, it was the Romans who finally put a stop to the self-destruction of the Jews.

Josephus says that Jerusalem, "went through greater agony before she fell...Her internal divisions destroyed the city, but the Romans destroyed the internal divisions." (War. V, 257) The Romans might well have blockaded the city and allowed the siege to drag on until the inhabitants were eventually starved into submission or destroyed themselves. In fact the more cautious of his advisers actually urged this on Titus when he called a council of war at the beginning of the siege.

It may have seemed pointless to wage war against those who were already destroying each other, but Titus also thought it unwise to let his army remain idle. Beside, "reputations were won by speed, (War. V, 499) so the Romans decided to fight their way into the city and bring the war as swiftly as possible to an end. Tacitus confirms that, "It seemed beneath them to wait for hunger to do its work on the enemy, and the troops actually asked to be allowed to risk their lives. Some did so because they had real courage, many from mere bravado and a desire for rewards. As for Titus, his imagination dwelt on Rome, wealth and pleasure: it would be long before these dreams were realized if Jerusalem were destined not to fall in the immediate future." (Tacitus. Histories.V11)

Nevertheless, the Romans could not have captured such a strongly fortified city if its defender had not fallen into a panic. When a small section of the north wall had been penetrated, Josephus tells us, "There was an immediate flight from the battlements, and even the party chiefs were filled with terror unjustified by the situation: Before the enemy got through they were stunned and ready to flee, and men once arrogant and bragging about their ungodly deed could be seen abject and trembling, insomuch that even in these vile scoundrels it was pitiful to note the change." False rumors that the whole west wall was down, or that the Romans were just around the corner, caused them to, "fall on their faces bewailing their own insane folly." (War. VI, 324-397)

"What happened would serve as an object lesson," Josephus wrote, "showing both the power of God over the wicked and the luck of the Romans. For the party chiefs divested themselves of their safety, and of their own accord came down from the towers on which they never have been subdued by force but only by starvation; and the Romans, who had toiled so hard to break through the weaker walls, captured by sheer luck those the engines could not touch; for no mechanical device could have made any impression of the three towers described elsewhere. Abandoning these, or rather driven from them by God, they took refuge for a moment in the ravine below Siloam." (War. VI, 399-401)

Thus were the days of the great tribulation shortened by what was conceded to be an act of God, not only by Josephus but also by Titus. Neither was aware that Jesus had predicted this very thing nearly forty years earlier.

The Destruction of the Temple

In the original prophecy of Daniel regarding the abomination of desolation, it was written, "For the overspreading of abominations he shall make it desolate," (9:27) and, "the people of the prince that shall come shall destroy the city and the sanctuary." (9:26) Within three weeks of the cessation of the daily sacrifice, the Romans, after setting fire to the gates, broke through into the Temple. It had not been the intention of Titus to burn down the sanctuary itself, but a Roman soldier flung a burning piece of wood through an aperture, and his fellows refused any attempt to put the fire out. (War. VI, 252-253)

Thus, Daniel's prophecy was literally fulfilled which said, "the people of the prince," not the prince himself, "shall destroy the city and the sanctuary: and the end thereof shall be with a flood, and unto the end of the war desolations are determined." (18:26) While the Temple itself was burning, looting went on all over Jerusalem, and in the following weeks the whole city was set on fire and destroyed. Josephus records that apart from three strong towers and a stretch of the west wall reserved as protection for the Roman garrison, "all the rest of the fortifications encircling the city were so completely levelled with the ground that no one visiting the spot would believe it had once been inhabited." (War. VII, 3)

Much of the city's great wealth had been buried or hidden in the sewers by the Jews. Consequently the looters were obliged to dig up the foundations of the Temple to get at the plunder." (War. VII, 115; VII, 375) This fulfilled Christ's prophecy that, "there shall not be left one stone upon another that shall not be thrown down." (Luke 21:6) As for the surrounding district, the Romans, when gathering timber for their siege platforms, had already stripped bare all the neighborhood for eleven or twelve miles. (War. V, 523; VI, 375-379)

The countryside, wrote Josephus, "like the city, was a pitiful sight; for where there once had been a lovely vista of woods and parks there was now nothing but desert and stumps of trees. No one - not even a foreigner - who had seen the old Judaea and the glorious suburbs of the city, and now set eyes on her present desolation, could have helped sighing and groaning at so terrible a change; for every trace of beauty had been blotted out by the war, and nobody who had known it in the past and came upon it suddenly would have recognized the place; when he was already there, he would still have been looking for the city." (War. VI, 6-8) As Daniel had predicted, "He shall make it desolate."

The Jews Slaughtered

Jesus, continuing His discourse, said that after the great tribulation, "They shall fall by the edge of the sword, and shall be lead away captive into all the nations." (Luke 21:24) In these words, He again pronounced the curse of God on rebellion as proclaimed by Moses many centuries earlier: "I will scatter you among the heathen, and will draw out a sword after you: and your land shall be desolate and your cities waste." (Lev. 26:33) Josephus estimated that over a million Jews perished during the siege of Jerusalem, and that all the prisoners taken during the war amounted to 97,000." (War. VI, 420)

We learn from Josephus that on the very day that the Romans broke in the city, a false prophet, "had declared to the people in the city that God commanded them to go into the Temple to receive the signs of their deliverance." Consequently a crowd of some six thousand, including women and children, had gathered on a colonnade. When the Romans set fire to it from below, they all perished in the flames.

After the city fell, Titus had all the insurgent terrorists executed, but the rest of the people, great numbers were allocated for exhibition, where they were slain either by the sword or wild beasts as entertainment. Most of those over seventeen, "were put in irons and sent to hard labor in Egypt. (War. VI, 418)

Again we see a penalty for disobedience pronounced by Moses, "and the Lord shall bring thee into Egypt again with ships, by the way whereof I spake unto thee; and there ye shall be sold unto your enemies for bondmen and bondwomen, and no man shall buy you." (Deut. 28:68) During the Exodus, the Israelites had marched out of Egypt overland, but now they were going back in ships. Although Josephus does not say that these captives were bought as slaves in Egypt, he does say that in other provinces, "those under seventeen were sold."

The war was not over in A.D. 70, however, for the Romans required a further three years to round up pockets of resistance in fortresses at Herodism in southern Judaea, Machaerus, east of the Dead Sea, and finally at Masada. Seventeen hundred Jews were massacred at Machaerus, and three thousand who had escaped from there and Jerusalem were surrounded and slaughtered in the Forest of Jardes. (War. VII, 210-214)

Not long after the fall of Jerusalem, there arose in north Africa, Johnathan, the weaver who persuaded a crowd of Jews to listen to him, "and led them out into the desert promising to show them signs and portents." (War. VII, 438-450) They were, however, soon rounded up, but the incident gave the Roman governor an excuse to murder three thousand of the wealthier Jews, while Johnathan, having been sent to Rome, was tortured and then burnt alive. Christians warned by Christ's prophecy would have been careful to avoid associating themselves with this man or his followers.

At Masada nine hundred and sixty perished in a final suicide pact when the Romans were about to force an entry. (War. VII, 401) Josephus puts into the mouth of Eleazar, commander of the Masada garrison, a list of Jewish colonies that had already been wiped out in other places, such as Caesarea and Scythopolis, adding that, "of all the towns in Syria there isn't one that hasn't exterminated its Jewish inhabitants." Damascus alone, had butchered 18,000 Jews with their wives and families. "As for those tortured to death in Egypt, it was stated that the number was something over 60,000." (War. VII, 367 f.)

Josephus says that the commander of Masada attributed all this to the vengeance of God, and said, "We ought perhaps to have read the mind of God and realized that His once beloved Jewish race had been sentenced to extinction...These things are God's vengeance for the many wrongs that in our madness we dared to do to our own country men...Long ago, it seems, God issued this warning to the whole Jewish race together, that life would be taken from us if we misused it." (War. VII, 327, 332) For this reason, he said, they were not to, "give the Romans the credit for the fact we are all ruined by the war against them; it is not through their power that these things have happened - mightier hand has intervened to give them the outward shape of victory." (War. VII, 359 f)

Thus, we have seen that when Jesus predicted that the Temple would be destroyed so that one stone should not be left standing on another, He not only gave His disciples signs that would precede this, but He indicated how great would be the tribulation that would accompany the event. These predictions were made in A.D. 33, and were recorded in writing by Matthew, Mark and Luke long before the Jewish War. If these gospels had been written after A.D. 70, the Gospel writers would have contained some statement confirming that the prophecy had been fulfilled.

Our principal source of information relating to these times has been the historian Josephus. Although he makes no allusion to our Lord's prophetic discourse, as a non-Christian, it is unlikely that he even knew of its existence. Nevertheless, he indicates in several passages in his history of the Jews that their sufferings and the desolation of Jerusalem were to be attributed to the vengeance of God in fulfillment of His purposes declared in the Old Testament Law. But Josephus also bears testimony to the special mercy of God in shortening days of suffering in Jerusalem at the end of the siege, a point not mentioned in the Old Testament, and first predicted by Jesus Himself.

Evidence that the prophecy was already in existence and well known to the Christian community before the outbreak of the war in A.D. 66 is provided by the fact that a large section of the Christian community evacuated the city and fled to Palla before it was too late. The subsequent source of events could only have confirmed the faith of those who heeded Christ's warning. In fact, Eusebius, in his History of the Church, written at the beginning of the fourth century, makes several pages of quotations from Josephus to demonstrate the accuracy of our Lord's prophecy.

In particular, Eusebius mentions the Abomination of Desolation announced by the prophets as having had its fulfillment, and he quotes Matthew 21:23-24 concerning the, "great distress in the land," as having been fully described by Josephus. He concludes that , "anyone who compared our Saviour's words with the rest of the historian's account of the whole war could not fail to be astonished, and to acknowledge as divine and utterly marvellous the foreknowledge revealed by our Saviour's prediction." (Eusebius, Church History III, 7)

Seeing then that it was fully recognized by the Christian church at this time, and for several centuries afterwards, that our Lord's prophecy of the great tribulation was fulfilled in the Jewish War, we may well ask on what grounds a certain section of the church today regards this event as future? Roman church history indicates that even Pope Gregory I, (590-604), the originator of much of the Roman Catholic dogma, taught that the great tribulation was to be associated with the future reign of a personal Antichrist. This view was rejected by all the Protestant Reformers, many of whom agreed with Eusebius and the early church.

disinfo - Paul and John were scribes to "the early church," and it is through them that we know of a still future "abomination of desolation."

The Bar Cochba Revolt

About sixty years after the destruction of Jerusalem, there arose a Jew named Bar Cochba, claiming to be the Messiah. He threatened Christians in particular that they would be, "sentenced to terrible punishments if they did not deny Christ and blaspheme him." (War. VI, 283-285) At that time, about the year 130, the emperor Hadrian, during a tour of his eastern provinces, had decided to found a new Roman city on the site of Jerusalem, and to erect a temple to Jupiter where formerly the Temple had stood. The ceremonial ploughing of the site in preparation for this, gave rise, in early 132, to a revolt of the residue of the Jews remaining in the land, who still cherished the hope that Jerusalem and a Temple would be rebuilt. (Schurer, History of the Jewish People, Vol. II, 291, 303)

The rebels soon took possession of the ruined site of Jerusalem and minted coins bearing the words, "Year One of the Redemption of Israel" and, "Year Two of the Freedom of Israel," while other coins, thought to belong to the third year, have only the words, "Of the Freedom of Jerusalem." The Roman governor, Rufus, was unable to cope with the situation with the forces at his disposal, and sent for reinforcements. When they arrived under the command of Julius Severus, a general recalled from Britain, the Jews were brought under control. (Dio Cassius, History, 69, 13) The climax of the war ended in Betthera, a little town not far from Jerusalem, after a blockade that lasted so long that hunger and thirst brought the revolutionaries to complete destruction, and the instigator of crazy folly paid the penalty he deserved. (Eusebius, Church History IV, 6)

Concluding his report on the Bar Cochba revolt, Eusebius says, "From that time on the entire race has been forbidden to set foot anywhere in the neighborhood of Jerusalem under the terms and ordinances of the law of Hadrian, which ensured that not even from a distance might Jews have a view of their ancestral soil...When in this way the city was closed to the Jewish race and suffered total destruction of its former inhabitants, it was colonized by an alien race, and the Roman city which subsequently arose, changed its name, so that now, in honour of the emperor then reigning, Aelius Hadrianus, it is known as Aelia." (Eusebius, Church History, IV, 6)

Thus the exile of the Jews and the obliteration of Jerusalem was completed. Years later, the very name had been so forgotten that when a Palestine Christian, on being asked from what city he came, had replied, "from Jerusalem," neither the governor nor any of his assistants knew where that was. (Eusebius, Martyrs of Palestine, 11) Jerusalem again resumed its name in the fourth century during the reign of the first Christian emperor, Constantine and the Church of the Holy Sepulchre was built on the site of a chapel dedicated to Venus. (Gibbon, Decline and Fall of the Roman Empire, Vol. III, p. 383)

Although the Jews were still refused entry on account of the hostility of Gentile Christians, Constantine's nephew, Julian, so disliked the Christian religion that when he became emperor in 362, he showed favor to the Jews as a mark of disrespect for Christianity. He published a letter in which he expressed concern for their former ill treatment, and canceled the taxes levied on them.

Finally, Julian promised that, "When I have successfully concluded the war with Persia, I will rebuild with my own efforts, the sacred city of Jerusalem, which for so many years you have longed to see inhabited, and bring settlers therein." (Works of Julian, Vol. III, p.22) Christian writers of the time report that this announcement was greeted with great enthusiasm by the Jews who not only subscribed financially, but offered their personal services in carrying out the enterprise.

The Roman historian Ammianus Marcellinus, who accompanied Julian on his expedition against Persia, also related that,

"He planned a vast cost to restore the once splendid temple at Jerusalem," which had been stormed and destroyed by Vespasian and Titus. For this purpose he commissioned Alypius of Antioch, formerly a vice-prefect in Britain, to carry out the work. He goes on to say, "though this Alypius pursued the work with vigour aided by the governor of the province, terrifying balls of flame made the place inaccessible to the workmen, some of whom burned to death; and since in this way the elements persistently repelled them, the enterprise halted." (Ammianus Marcellinus, XXIII, i, 2-3)

It is not necessary to believe in supernatural balls of fire. It is well known that Jerusalem was riddled with sewers and other underground works in which the Jews had taken refuge when Jerusalem fell. It is quite possible that explosive gases may have accumulated there. When work on the new foundations for the Temple began, these gases would be released and could have been ignited by those exploring the tunnels with lighted torches. Afterwards, superstition and rumor may have embellished the original story.

Whether or not Marcellinus' record is true, the fact remains that the Roman emperor, did on more than one occasion announce his intention of rebuilding the Temple and restoring the Jews to Jerusalem. It is believed by ancient historians that it was his hostility to Christianity and not because he liked the Jews that motivated him. And in doing so he would be nullifying Christ's prophecy and so discredit the Christian faith. (Gibbon, Vol. III p. 384) But Julian's plans were never completed, for although his Persian campaign was a military success, he himself was killed, thus bringing his brief reign of only twenty months to an abrupt end. (Gibbon, Vol. IV, p. 442)

Another attempt at Jewish restoration was made in the year 614, when Chosroes II, King of Persia, invaded the eastern territories of the Roman empire. When he threatened Palestine, the Jews of Syria and the Phoenician coast rose in his support, and an army of some 15,000 marched to aid his conquest of the Holy

Land and Jerusalem. Arriving on the outskirts of the city, they set about plundering and burning the Christian churches. Later, when the Persians entered the city, they took captive many thousands of Christians whom they sold to the Jews who wished to take vengeance on them. Every Christian church was demolished, and their treasures carried off to Persia. (Gibbon, Vol. IV, p.511)

However, the dream of a Jewish restoration under Persian protection was short. Fifteen years later, in 629, the emperor Horaclius drove the Persian out, and recovered most of the spoil. (Gibbon, Vol. IV, p. 533)

The Romans did not remain long in possession, for in 637 Jerusalem was captured by the Arab followers of Mahamet led by Caliph Omar who declared Jerusalem a holy city second only to Mecca. He then built a house of prayer on the Temple site.

Half a century later the Caliph Abdul Malik built the Dome of the Rock which stands today on the summit of the mountain where formerly the Temple altar of sacrifice had stood. At first, the Arab Moslems remained tolerant to the western Christian church and the Jews, but in 1071 the Soljuk Turks, advancing from central Asia, overthrew the eastern Roman empire and captured Jerusalem. Moslem persecution of Christians then led to the Crusades, and the Crusaders, who were mainly Franks under papal influence who held Jerusalem from 1099 till 1187, when they were expelled by Saladin, Sultan of Egypt.

Apart from a brief period between 1229 and 1244, when the Crusaders recaptured the city, Jerusalem remained in Egyptian hands until 1517, when the Ottoman Turks conquered both Palestine and Egypt. The Sultan of Turkey at that time acquired the title of Caliph, or nominal head of all Moslems, and Jerusalem remained in Turkish hands until 1917. On Nov. 2 of that year, it was announced by the British government that after the war, part of Palestine should become a national home for the Jews.

The Turks were driven out of Palestine by a British and Commonwealth force in a campaign that began in October 1917.

On December 9, the Turks vacated Jerusalem and two days later General Allenby made his official entry and received its surrender. This occurred 2520 years, to within a matter of days, after Jehoiakim submitted to the rule of Nebuchadnezzar in Kislev, 604 B.C. The general principles of this prophetic interpretation had been published by Dr. Grattan Guinness in 1886 together with the terminal date of 1917, almost half a century earlier. This should be regarded as a clear vindication of the historicist interpretation held by the Protestant Reformers. But today, this view of prophecy has been almost universally neglected by the leading denominations and few, if any, theologians are aware of these significant historical dates, or the manner in which the time period has worked out.

Signs In The Sun and Moon

We read in Matthew 24:29-30, "Immediately after the tribulation of those days shall the sun be darkened, and the moon shall not give her light, and the stars shall fall from heaven, and the powers of the heavens shall be shaken. Then shall appear the sign of the Son of man in heaven: and then shall all the tribes of the earth mourn, and they shall see the Son of man coming in the clouds of heaven with power and great glory."

The signs in the sun, moon and stars are thus seen to be the first important signs of the Second Advent for which the disciples had asked. We note that these signs follow, "immediately after the tribulation of those days." Many readers have jumped to the conclusion that the tribulation mentioned here is the same as the great tribulation described earlier in verse 21, but there is not the slightest justification for this. We have already seen that the great tribulation in verse 21 and 22 apply in every respect to the Jewish war of A.D. 66-70.

Following the prophecy of the great tribulation, Matthew's version foresaw the appearance of false Christs and false prophets until finally the Son of man Himself would be seen as plainly as lightning is visible from east to west. Viewed in this context, "the tribulation of those days," must refer to the other tribulation in the days preceding the Second Advent. Luke's version of the prophecy omits the words, "immediately after the tribulation of those days," and gives only a summary of the astronomical phenomena.

Many students of Bible prophecy are aware that those signs of the sun, moon and stars are not be be taken literally, but as

unbeliever

symbolic. They are employed symbolically in both the Old and New Testament prophecies. In the Creation story the sun and moon denote rulers, for the sun is said to rule the day, and the moon to rule the night. (Gen. 1:16) In Joseph's dream in which he saw the sun, moon and stars bow down to him, (Gen. 37:9) Jacob took this to mean himself, Rachel and Joseph's brothers.

So in the prophecies, the heavenly bodies, or heavens denote the ruling powers of the world, the sun representing the supreme power, or head of state, while the moon and stars denote the secondary of lesser powers. Isaiah employed this language when he predicted the overthrow of Babylon by the Medes. The downfall of their rulers were described as, "The stars of heaven and the constellations thereof shall not give their light: the sun shall be darkened in his going forth. and the moon shall not cause her light to shine." (Isa. 13:10) The destruction of Idumea is foretold in similar terms. (Isa. 34:4)

Again in Ezekiel's prophecy of the downfall of Egypt made about 585 B.C., just after the fall of Jerusalem, we read, "I will cover the heaven and make the stars thereof dark; I will cover the sun with a cloud, and the moon shall not give light. All the bright lights of heaven will I make dark over thee, and set darkness upon thy land, saith the Lord God." (Ezek. 32:7-8) The first stage in the fulfillment of this prophecy came five or six years later when the reigning Pharaoh Apries (Biblical Hophra, Jew. 44:30) and his regime were overthrown by an army general named Amasis.

Although Amasis is said to have been of, "humble and undistinguished origin, he reigned over Egypt for more than forty years. Ezekiel's plain language prophecy, made in 570 B.C., came true in 525 B.C. at the battle of Pelusium in which the Egyptians were defeated by the Persians and Cambyses, the Persian king and his successors became rulers of Egypt. The so-called Twenty-seventh Dynasty of Pharaohs consisted, in fact, of the kings of Persia, and since that time no native-born Egyptian has ever reigned in that land.

From these, and other examples in Joel 2:10, 31; Rev. 6:12-16; and 8:12, it is evident that such signs are neither astronomical nor peculiar to the end of the world. (age) <u>The darkening of the sun and moon is not to be taken literally</u>, but as symbolizing the fall of great political powers and rulers. Watch and see

When the signs in the Lord's prophecy are considered in this way, they appear to indicate that the political powers ruling over Jerusalem and the Holy Land would suffer extinction immediately after World War I, and this is exactly what happened to the Moslem powers. The principal Caliph at the time was the Sultan of Turkey who also held office as Caliph, nominally religious leader of all Moslems. As history shows us, shortly after the war, the Sultan was deposed in 1922 when Turkey became a republic and two years later the Caliphate was abolished altogether.

The downfall of those Moslem powers is, no doubt, the principal application of the prophecy, but we should not overlook the fact that at the same time, other monarchies were falling in Europe. These included the Tsarist regime in Russia, the Kaiser in Germany, while in Austria the Hapsburg empire also disintegrated. All this political disruption may be included in the words of Jesus recorded in Matthew: "The stars shall fall from heaven, and the powers of the heavens shall be shaken." (24:29)

Luke's version of the prophecy says, "There shall be signs in the sun, and in the moon, and in the stars: and upon the earth distress of nations with perplexity: the sea and the waves roaring; men's hearts failing them for fear, and for looking after those things which are coming on the earth: for the powers of heaven shall be shaken." (Luke 21:26)

The sea is a prophetic symbol for, "peoples, and multitudes, and nations, and tongues." (Rev. 17:15)

The political unrest envisioned in this passage accompanies and follows the signs in the sun, moon and stars, and must extend also to the Second World War and beyond. The invention of atomic and nuclear weapons in modern times has given rise to fears that if such weapons were used in modern times it could lead to the extinction of the entire human race, and make the whole earth uninhabitable. It is probably true to say that there has never been a time when there has been so much perplexity about the future of mankind.

Daniel's Seventy Weeks

One of the most remarkable prophecies in the Bible concerning Jerusalem is attributed to Daniel and recorded by him. It is made up of statements made by the angel Gabriel who was specifically commissioned to give information to Daniel who had been interceding earnestly for Jerusalem to be delivered from its desolation. Daniel was also concerned with the coming of the Messiah and the end of the age. Gabriel commenced by saying to Daniel:

"Seventy weeks are determined upon thy people and upon the holy city, to finish the transgression, and to make an end of sins, and to make reconciliation for iniquity, and to bring in everlasting righteousness, and to seal up the vision and prophecy, and to anoint the most Holy. Know therefore and understand, that from the going forth of the commandment to restore and to build Jerusalem unto the Messiah the Prince shall be seven weeks, and threescore and two weeks: the street shall be built again, and the wall, even in troublous times." (Dan. 9:24-25)

Isaiah, prophesying of the same event says that Cyrus, king of Persia would make a decree, "saying to Jerusalem, Thou shalt be built; and to the temple, Thy foundation shall be laid." (44:28) But in the decree only the restoration of the Temple is mentioned, not the city. (Ezra 1:1-4) In accordance with this part of the decree, the Temple was completed in the sixth year of Darius-third day of Adar. (Ezra 6:15) No attempt was made to build the walls of Jerusalem until the reign of Artaxerxes. (405-424) (Ezra 4:11-12)

It appears, however, that although Cyrus had made a decree about Jerusalem as well as the Temple, the part referring to the city was not issued until Ezra returned from Babylon in the seventh year of Artaxerxes, that is in the spring of 458 B.C., (Ezra 7:1-9) and began work on the city and its walls. (Ezra 4:12) Now the interval between Ezra's return in 458 B.C. when apparently authorization was given to start work on the city, until A.D. 33, when Christ was crucified and completed His work of Atonement, is exactly four hundred and ninety years. It has been generally assumed, however, that the seventy weeks, or four hundred and ninety days are to be understood as symbolizing 490 years. The precision with which this period was complete should be suf-ficient reason to believe that this is the correct application to the prophecy.

In Daniel 9:27 are foretold the achievements of the Messiah: "And he shall confirm the covenant with many for one week and in the midst of the week he shall cause the sacrifice and oblation to cease." The covenant mentioned here is the New Covenant, the terms of which had already been announced by Jeremiah (31:31-34) and were now being ratified by the blood of Jesus Christ. (Heb. 8:5; 9:15) "In the midst of the week," that is when Jesus began His ministry in the autumn of A.D. 29, He offered up His life, saying, "Lo I come to do thy will, O God." (Heb. 10-9) Thus was fulfilled the symbolic burnt offering, the feature of the daily sacrifice. (Exod. 29:41)

Following Jesus' baptism, Oct. 14, A.D. 29, the sacrifice and oblation ceased to have any further validity, after He began His ministry, "in the midst of the week." The sacrifices for sin, how-ever, did not become void until He completed His work on the Cross at the end of the seventieth week, April 3, A.D. 33. It should be noted that Jesus offered Himself for sacrifice and was accepted, (His baptism) half a "week" (3 1/2 years) before the end of Daniel's 70 "weeks," or in other words, at the end of 69 1/2 prophetic "weeks" or 486 1/2 actual years. (586 1/2 - 457 3/4 = 28 3/4 Autumn A.D. 29)

Exactly in the midst of the 70th week, Christ caused sacrifice and oblation to cease, precisely as foretold five centuries before.

This is in full harmony with the statement in Daniel 9:26, that Messiah would be, "cut off, but not for himself." The sacrifice of Jesus, the Messiah, began when He was 30 years old and was completely consummated when he was 33 1/2 years old, thereby ending the 70th week of Daniel. The crucifixion of Christ, the Messiah, finished the transgression of the Jews as He was the only One who could have saved them. Peter condemned the Jews when he said: "But ye denied the Holy One and the Just, and desired a murderer to be granted unto you; you killed the Prince of life, whom God hath raised from the dead; whereof we are witnesses." (Acts 3:14-15) As a result of this denial of their Messiah the Prince, the House of Judah became equally responsible with the non-Israel Edomites (Jews) for the destruction of the city of Jerusalem and the burning of the Temple in 70 A.D., when the Roman armies accomplished this task of destruction.

Today, many Bible scholars and even ministers of the Scriptures have accepted and promote a false teaching of the futurist school of interpretation that the word "he" in Daniel 9:27 referred to, "the Anti-Christ," who makes his appearance after the saints are secretly caught up to meet Him in the air. In order to make the angel Gabriel substantiate their prognostications, they read the word "confirm" to read "make." The "he" in verse 26 is the same "he" who in verse 27 confirms the covenant.

It has always been accepted by the early church that Jesus Christ ended Daniel's 70th week at His Crucifixion in the spring of A.D. 33. But in the second quarter of the nineteenth century, J.N. Darby, a very young man with no academic training in theology founded the Brethren Movement. He persuaded his followers that within this period of forgiveness of sins all the Jewish people were to be made actually righteous.

Later when it became apparent that this was not happening, the fulfillment of a large part of the prophecy had to be relegated to some future date and the last part of the period was lopped off and held indefinitely in suspense. (the Gap Theory) In the last century this hitherto unheard interpretation was disseminated

This is the first time I've seen the Church Age refered to as "the Gap Theory." It usually refers to the time between Genesis 1:1 and 1:3

through the notes of the Scofield Reference Bible (1977 p. 222 f.) and a state of confusion and disagreement has been brought about by its acceptance in many evangelical churches. (E.R. Sandeen, The Roots of Fundamentalism)

The Sign of the Fig Tree

In all three gospels, after the verses predicting the Second Advent itself, there follows the parable of the fig tree. "Now learn a parable of the fig tree; When his branch is yet tender, and putteth forth leaves, ye know that summer is nigh: So likewise ye, when ye shall see all these things, know that it is near, even at the doors...Verily I say unto you, This generation shall not pass, till all these things be fulfilled." (Matt. 24:32-34) To understand the meaning of this parable of the fig tree, it is necessary to first learn the symbolic meaning of the tree.

Jesus taught in parable, often coached in symbolic language, not necessarily to make things easy for everyone to understand, but rather to hide from outsiders the secrets He wished to reveal only to His own people. (Matt. 13:10-17) During the last year of His ministry, Jesus had spoken a parable about a barren fig tree: "A certain man had a fig tree planted in his vineyard; and he came and sought fruit thereon, and found none. Then said he unto the dresser of his vineyard, Behold, these three years I come seeking fruit on this fig tree, and find none: cut it down; why cumbereth it the ground? And he answering said unto him, Lord, let it alone this year also, till I shall dig about it, and dung it: And if it bear fruit, well, and if not, then after that thou shalt cut it down." (Luke 13:6-9)

Most Bible scholars agree that the fig tree in the parable represents the Jews (Judah) to whom our Lord had then come three years seeking "fruit" in the form of repentance. The parable had its sequel a few days before the Crucifixion. On His way into Jerusalem, Jesus, "seeing a fig tree afar off having leaves, he came, if haply he might find any thing thereon: and when he came to it, he found nothing but leaves; for the time of figs was not yet. And

Jesus answered and said unto it, No man eat fruit of thee hereafter for ever." (Mark 11: 13-14)

On the following day as Jesus and his disciples went out of Jerusalem, "as they passed by, they saw the fig tree dried up from the roots. And Peter, calling to remembrance saith unto him, Master, behold, the fig tree which thou cursedst is withered away." (Mark 11: 20-21) Those who understand symbolism realize this was the final stage of Jesus' previous parable which he acted out, indicating that sentence had now been passed on the Jewish nation. Later He was to make it even more clear: "Therefore say I unto you. The kingdom of God shall be taken from you and given to a nation bringing forth the fruits thereof." (Matt. 21:43)

In view of the earlier parables, we may justifiably regard the fig tree as signifying the Jews in the parable concerning the Second Advent. After 1917 many Jews, mainly of non-Judah origin immigrated into the Holy Land, and on May 1948 became established as an independent nation, thus making their appearance in the political "heaven." Since then, it can be said they have been producing leaves but no fruit. If so, we can infer that the coming of Christ is near, "even at the door." (verse 33)

According to historical evidence, it appears that at least 85% of Jews today are proselytes with no blood connection with ancient Israel; in short, they are not true Jews of Judah. History also indicates there are over eleven million Ashkenazim Jews in the world who are descended from the Khazars, an Asian people who established a strong kingdom in what is now Southern Russia and, "who adopted Judaism during the 8th century." (Universal Jewish Encyclopedia, Vol. 6, p. 375) Also there is a strong element from rejected Esau (Zionists) who are not of God's chosen seed of Jacob, who are today the rulers of the world's finances and are sworn enemies of Christianity.

Yet the modern Jews are acknowledged throughout Christendom as representing the whole House of Jacob. This total misinterpretation of Scripture has brought confusion within the Church itself and loss of credibility among unbelievers world-wide. All these Jews have committed perhaps the most grievous sin of all in their vehement rejection of Jesus Christ, the Son of God, as Israel's promised Messiah. "You will understand me when I say to you that Jews cannot accept Jesus or anyone else as the one redeeming, atoning Son of God. We believe we have access to God without intermediary. Such is the teaching, implicit and explicit, of Israel (Jewry)." (Chief Rabbi Stephen S. Wise as quoted by "The Dispossessed Majority" p. 156)

The next statement Jesus made, "This generation shall not pass, till all these things shall be fulfilled. (Matt. 24:34) Following closely before the appearance of the Son of Man (v. 30) can only mean that the generation which sees the fig tree putting forth leaves but no fruit, will also see the return of Christ. In other words, verse 34 appears to indicate there will be people who are living in 1948, will be living and actually witness the coming of The Christ. However, no precise date for the Second Advent can be derived from this prophecy, for Jesus went on to say, "Of that day and hour knoweth no man, no, not the angels of heaven, but my Father only." (Matt. 24:36)

Paul, writing to the Thessalonians said, "Of the times and seasons, brethren ye have no need that I write unto you." (I Thess. 5:1) Paul may be acknowledging that they knew the time within broad limits, because Jesus had said, "When ye shall see all these things, know that it is near, even at the doors." A common teaching among Bible scholars today is that the coming of the Lord may occur, "at any moment," and in support several Scriptures are quoted, such as, "Behold I come as a thief," (Rev. 19:15) and, "Yourselves know perfectly that the day of the Lord cometh as a thief in the night. For when they shall say, Peace and safety, then sudden destruction cometh upon them, as travail upon a woman with child: and they shall not escape." (I Thess. 5:2-3; 2 Peter 3:10)

It is, of course, quite true that for the world in general, who are not Christians, the coming of Christ will be sudden and unexpected, for in the very next sentence Paul goes on to say, "But ye, brethren, are not in darkness, that that day should overtake you as a thief. Ye are the children of light and the children of the day: we are not of the night or of darkness." (I Thess. 5:4-5) If our Lord gave the Christian church in Jerusalem clearly recognizable signs when they were to flee to the mountains to escape the coming judgment, we must surely expect that He has given His own people today equally clear and unmistakable signs of His return to judge the world. But as the unbelieving Jews were trapped in Jerusalem, so today, unbelievers will be completely taken by surprise by the coming of Christ.

All three Gospel writers tell of the "Son of man" coming in the clouds of heaven: Matthew 24:30; Mark 13:26; and Luke 21:27. The statements about, "coming in the clouds," may allude to Daniel's vision, " I saw in the night visions and behold, one like the Son of man came with the clouds of heaven, and came to the Ancient of days, and they brought him near before him. And there was given him dominion, and glory, and a kingdom, that all people, nations, and languages, should serve him; his dominion is an everlasting dominion, which shall not pass away, and his kingdom shall not be destroyed." (Dan. 7:13-14)

By alluding to Daniel's vision in this way, our Lord evidently intended to remind His disciples of Daniel's prophecies. In the second chapter of Daniel, the kingdom of God is represented by a stone that strikes the feet of an image and destroys it. The image (of Nebuchadnezzar's dream) was made of various metals which represented the empires and governments of this world. The image's head was of fine gold, his breast and arms of silver, his belly of brass, his legs of iron, his feet part of iron and part of clay.

We are told that the first four parts of the image represent a succession of four kingdoms or empires that would rule the world. History identifies them as Babylon, Medo-Persia, Greece and Rome, which each in turn became the predominate power in the world and ruled over Palestine. The two legs of the image may well represent the dividing of the Roman Empire (the fourth kingdom) into two halves which took place in the year 395 A.D. And Eastern

Empire under Emperor Arcadius with its capital at Constantinople and a Western Empire under Emperor Honorius, retaining the capital at Rome. Together the two halves continued to be the dominant world power until the Roman Empires collapsed under the onslaught of the Turks following the rout of their armies at the battle of Manzikert in 1071 A.D.

In Nebuchadnezzar's dream the legs of the image represent the fourth kingdom (Rome) terminating in feet having ten toes, signifying the final subdivision of the Roman Empire, as it was at the time of its fall, around 476 A.D., into ten European sections. Since that time no single power has ever predominated as Daniel foretold, "but they shall not cleave one to another, even as iron is not mixed with clay." (Dan. 2:43)

According to Daniel's interpretation, the kingdom of God was to be set up, "in the days of those kings." The only kings mentioned in this chapter are those that represent the four empires, so we must conclude that the kingdom of God was to have its beginning during the existence of those empires or kingdoms. This evidently excludes the earthly kingdom of Israel which had been established under David long before the time of Nebuchadnezzar. In fact, Daniel clearly speaks of the founding of the kingdom as future in his day, as we read in Daniel 2:45: "A great God has made known to the king what shall be hereafter."

On the other hand, "in the days of those kings," required that the stone kingdom be founded before the fourth empire came to an end. Now John the Baptist proclaimed, and our Lord confirmed, that the kingdom of heaven is at hand. (Matt. 3:2,4,17) It was evidently founded during His lifetime for He also declared, reading from Luke 17:21: "The kingdom of God in heaven," is called either, "the kingdom of God" or "the kingdom of heaven."

Daniel's prophecy continues, "Thou sawest till a stone was cut out without hands, which smote the image upon his feet that were of iron and clay, and brake them to pieces, Then was the iron, the clay, the brass, the silver, and the gold, broken to pieces together and became like the chaff of the summer threshing floors; and the wind carried them away, that no place was found for them: and the stone that smote the image became a great mountain, and filled the whole earth." (Dan. 2:34-35)

In its interpretation (verse 44) it is explained that the stone represents, "a kingdom which shall never be destroyed: and the kingdom shall not be left to other people, but it shall break in pieces and consume all those kingdoms, and it shall stand for ever." The stone striking the feet of the image clearly depicts a sudden catastrophic event that has not yet taken place, for human forms of governments continue to rule the world. Since the stone struck the feet of the image, the event described could not have taken place until long after the Roman Empire had fallen.

During the present age, the kingdom of God is represented only by a stone as we read in Daniel 2:34: "cut out by no human hand," which implies the supernatural origin of the kingdom. This is seen in the virgin birth of Jesus Christ and His miraculous resurrection from the dead. Scripturally, the stone symbolizes Jesus Christ, for our Lord Himself said, "Did ye never read in the scriptures, The stone the builders rejected, the same is become the head of the corner: This is the Lord's doing, and it is marvellous in our eyes." (Matt. 21:42)

It is not until after the image was smashed that the stone, as we read in Dan. 2:35, "became a great mountain, and filled the whole earth." This is also foretold in Revelation 11:15, "The kingdoms of this world are become the kingdoms of our Lord, and of his Christ; and he shall reign for ever and ever." It is generally believed by Bible scholars this will come about when Jesus Christ returns to judge the world and establish His Kingdom on earth as it is in heaven." This is not a kingdom in the sky. The idea that the kingdom of heaven is a spirit world, to be vaguely thought of as existing somewhere in outer space, is a piece of Greek philosophy. Such an idea has no Scriptural foundation.

The Period of Gentile Domination

In speaking of the kingdoms of this world, our Lord seemed to imply that in the divine plan of God, a definite period of time had been foreseen for the period of Gentile domination of Jerusalem. This was linked with a similar period allocated to the Gentiles.

In 1823, an American, John A. Brown, in his Even-Tide, (p.xlii f.) believed that this period had been given in Daniel chapter 4 as the "seven times" mentioned in verses 16, 25, and 32. Thus when the tree was hewn down, leaving only a stump in the earth, (v. 23) Nebuchadnezzar had been told that, "they shall make thee to eat grass as oxen, and they shall wet thee with the dew of heaven, and seven times shall pass over thee, till thou know that the most high ruleth in the kingdom of men, and giveth it to whomsoever He will. (v. 25) John Brown supposed that the ending of this period would see the beginning of the millennium, but there is nothing in the prophecy to indicate this.

Although it has been widely supposed that the "seven times" meant seven years in Nebuchadnezzar's case, a "time" when used as a unit in Bible prophecy, is not the same as a year, but is only three hundred and sixty days. This figure is derived from the prophecies in Revelation chapter twelve where we read of the women who fled into the wilderness for a period of 1260 days (v. 6) but three and a half "times" in verse 14. Doubling these figures gives us "seven times" as equal to the 1260 days in verse 6. Then if a day symbolizes a year, as we saw in the case of Daniel's Seventy Weeks prophecy, the "seven times" would symbolize 2520 years.

On the assumption that Nebuchadnezzar began his reign in 604 B.C., John Brown calculated that the times of the Gentiles

Nebuchadnezzar was restored to the throne after 7 literal years

would end in 1917. Later, other nineteenth century scholars, notably, Dr. H. Grattan Guinness, (Light for the Last Days, 1886, p. 346) made similar calculations. A series of tablets recovered from the ruins of Nineveh, known as the Babylonian Chronicles, in more recent times has thrown much light on the circumstances and date of the subjugation of Jerusalem by Nebuchadnezzar.

Following the Babylonian victory over an Egyptian army at Carchenish on the Euphrates during the summer of 605 B.C., Nebuchadnezzar threatened Jerusalem at the time when his army was chasing the fleeing Egyptians through Palestine. There is no evidence that Jerusalem was captured on this occasion, although Daniel and other hostages were carried away captive to Babylon (Daniel 1:1-6) (L.J. Wiseman, Chronicles of Chaldean Kings, 1950, p.26).

In the following year Nebuchadnezzar returned, and all the rulers of the Mediterranean lands, including Jehoiakim, king of Judah, submitted to his yoke. (p. 28) The Chronicles tell us that Nebuchadnezzar received tribute from these kings in the month of Kislev, (p. 69, lines 10-13) that is about November or December, 604 B.C. This dates the record of II Kings 24:1 which says, "In his days, Nebuchadnezzar, king of Babylon came up, and Jehoiakim became his servant three years; then he turned and rebelled against him."

Nebuchadnezzar's defeat in Egypt in 601 (p. 29, p. 71, lines 5-7) three years later, would provide the opportunity for this rebellion. This must be regarded as the first and principal date when Jerusalem came under Gentile domination. Jehoiakim however, was allowed to remain king until he was succeeded by his son Jehoiachin. (II Kings 24:6) Owing to the latter's hostility to Babylon, Nebuchadnezzar again invaded Palestine early in 597 B.C. and removed Jehoiachin, appointing Zedekiah in his place as puppet king. The Babylonian Chronicles give the date of this as the second day of the month Adar, equivalent to March 16, 597 B.C. (p. 33, 73, line 11)

However, if we use 604 B.C. as a starting point, Seven Times, or 2520 years, we come to 1917 A.D. and the capture of Jerusalem by the British forces under General Edmund Allenby. This ended the Seven Times period of Gentile domination. Even the day and the month of Jerusalem's deliverance was recorded by the little known prophet Haggai. He said it would be the 24th day of the Hebrew month Kislev, which for the year 1917 fell on December 9th the exact day Jerusalem fell to General Allenby. (As Birds Flying, Andrew Adams, 1992) God is always faithful to His promises and prophecies – with only a few remaining to be fulfilled.

Signs of the Second Advent

In His discourse on the mount of Olives, Jesus gave clear signs of when the Temple would be destroyed, having already predicted that one stone would not be left standing on another. He then foretold the exile of the Jews and the treading down of Jerusalem by the Gentiles till their times were fulfilled. We have seen the domination of Jerusalem by the Gentiles brought to an end in the First World War. Immediately after that war we saw the downfall of the powers which had ruled over Jerusalem, namely the Sultan of Turkey and the Moslem Caliphate, thus fulfilling the symbolic prophecy that, "Immediately after the tribulation of those days shall the sun be darkened and the moon shall not give her light." (Matt. 24:29) Finally in 1948 we have seen the birth of the Jewish nation symbolized by the fig tree putting forth leaves. From these signs many who study Bible prophecy today have realized that the return of Jesus Christ must be near, "even at the doors."

We have now come to the final great sign which the whole world will find impossible to ignore, "And then shall appear the sign of the Son of man in heaven: and then shall all the tribes of the earth mourn, and they shall see the Son of man coming in the clouds of heaven with great power and glory." (Matt. 24:30) All the, "signs of the times," are only the forerunners of this final sign which will be the conclusive proof that the, "time of the end," had come. All previous signs are merely warnings of its approach: to take heed when it does come will be too late.

Skeptics and disbelievers in the Bible will probably say His sign in the heaven will be some unusual astronomical sign and will not be expecting the, "sign of the Son of Man," to be the actual appearance of Christ Himself. The Scriptures tell us in the plainest words, "Behold, he cometh with the clouds: and every eye shall see him, and they also which pierced him and all kindred of the earth shall wail because of him. Even so, Amen." It is therefore no invisible or intangible spirit who is to return, but the same Jesus who appeared to the disciples after the Resurrection and said, "A spirit hath not flesh and bones, as ye see me have." (Luke 24:39) Later He invited the doubting Thomas to, "reach hither thy finger, and behold my hands, and reach higher thy hand, and thrust it into my side." (John 20:27)

Could anything be plainer than the words addressed to the apostles who witnessed His ascension? "While they beheld, He was taken up; and a cloud received Him out of their sight. And while they looked steadfastly toward Heaven as He went up, behold two men stood by them in white apparel; which also said, Ye men of Galilee, why stand ye gazing up into Heaven? This same Jesus, which is taken up from you into heaven, shall so come in like manner as ye have seen him go into heaven." (Acts 1: 9-11)

There are many today who cannot realize the possibility of such an event happening in this materialistic, commercialized world of today, even if they do not go so far as to deny it altogether. Those who read the Bible can picture Christ, like any other Palestinian of His day, nineteen centuries ago, walking the streets of Jerusalem or conversing with its inhabitants; they can almost imagine that, but for Him to appear suddenly in the midst of our great modern cities appears to them too fantastic for serious contemplation. Such an entire and absolute change in the established constitution and government of the nations of the world would be considered not merely unlikely but too incredible to imagine.

Even as Christ's first coming was both expected and unexpected, so will His second coming be. There were those who watched and waited for Him over nineteen centuries ago, and who, consequently were ready to receive Him when He came. Again there were others, the great majority, who had no such expectation in spite of what the Scriptures told them. It is the same today. There are some who look for the Lord's return, but there are others, by far the greater number, who are on the lookout for anything and everything rather than that great event.

Luke 17:24-25 tells us what must take place prior to the Second Advent. "For as the lightning, that lighteneth out of the one part under heaven, shineth unto the other part under heaven: so shall also the Son of man be in his day. But first must suffer many things, and be rejected of this generation." Isaiah also declared, "The glory of the Lord shall be revealed, and all flesh shall see it together." (Isa. 40:5) We see that our Lord gave no support to the idea that the kingdom of God had already come to the early Christian church.

A total perversion of scripture. Not "have strength" which would put the onus on us, but to be "accounted worthy," which puts the onus on God, who does the accounting!

The Second Advent

The purpose of His coming the Second time, after a long absence, will be to judge and sweep away man's worldly systems of government and establish His own righteous kingdom. Luke gives a warning of the judgments that are to take place at that time. "Take heed to yourselves lest your hearts be weighed down with dissipation and drunkenness and cares of this life, and that day come upon you suddenly like a snare; for it will come upon all who dwell upon the face of the whole earth. But watch at all times, praying that you may <u>have strength</u> to <u>escape</u> all these things that will take place, and to stand before the Son of man." (Luke 21:34-36 RSV) *What stupidity*

<u>There is no suggestion here</u> that some people are going to avoid the times of trouble and the judgments by being transported to heaven while they take place. Unpleasant things are already happening today, and they may well get worse, "Men's hearts failing them for fear, and for looking after those things that are coming on the earth." (Luke 21:26) But our Lord said, "When these things begin to come to pass, then look up, and lift up your heads, for your redemption draweth nigh." (verse 28) <u>We are encouraged to watch and pray that we may have the strength to endure them, not to avoid them.</u> *Perverse versions (RSV) produce perverse persons.*

Just as Noah had foreknowledge when the flood was to come, so may Christians have an approximate knowledge when the day of judgment may be expected. But as for the rest of mankind, "as in the days that were before the flood they were eating and drinking, marrying and giving in marriage, until the day that Noah entered into the ark, and knew not until the flood came, and took them all away; so shall also the coming of the Son of man be." (Matt. 24:37-39)

In Matthew's account of the prophecies of Jesus he recorded these words:

"Immediately after the tribulation of those days shall the sun be darkened, and the moon shall not give her light and the stars shall fall from heaven, and the powers of the heavens shall be shaken." (Matt. 24:29) This is followed (as in the other gospels) by the actual coming of the "Son of man in the clouds of heaven with power and great glory." (v. 30) Thus we find the first important sign of the Second Advent for which the disciples had asked.

Because the signs in the sun and moon follow, "immediately after the tribulation of those days," many scholars have jumped to the conclusion that the tribulation mentioned here is the same as the great tribulation described earlier in Matthew 24:21, a tribulation clearly applicable to the Jewish War of A.D. 70. The tribulation of verse 29 (prefaced in a new paragraph in the King James text) must refer to another tribulation occurring in the days preceding the Second Advent. Luke's version of this prophecy omits the words, "immediately after the tribulation of those days," and gives only a summary of the astronomical phenomena.

Because His disciples thought that the kingdom of God should immediately appear, (Luke 19:11-37) Jesus spoke two parables that referred to the Second Advent; Both give no support to the idea that the kingdom of God had already come in the founding of the Christian church.

Parable One: The Ten Virgins

Matthew 25: 1-13 tells of the, "ten virgins which took their lamps and went forth to meet the bridegroom." Reading from the Amplified Bible: "Five of them were foolish - thoughtless, without forethought; and five were wise – sensible, intelligent and prudent. For when the foolish took their lamps, they did not take any (extra) oil with them; But the wise took flasks of oil along with them (also) with their lamps. While the bridegroom lingered and was slow in coming, they all began nodding their heads and fell asleep. But at midnight there was a shout, Behold the bridegroom! Go out to meet him! Then all those virgins got up and put their own lamps in order. And the foolish said to the wise, Give us some of your oil, for our lamps are going out. But the wise replied, There will not be enough for us and for you; go instead to the dealers and buy for yourselves. But while they were gone away to buy, the bridegroom came, and those who were prepared went in with him to the marriage feast; the door was shut. Later the other virgins also came, and said, Lord open (the door) to us! But He replied, I solemnly declare to you, I do not know you - I am not acquainted with you."

A popular assumption is that the foolish virgins are the unsaved but this cannot be the case. The question of salvation is not mentioned in the parable. The ten virgins were all His friends or they would not have been invited to the marriage. They all had waited a long time for His arrival and had fallen asleep. They knew it would be a night arrival and had not expected it to be delayed so long. The five virgins who did not have an extra supply of oil besides what was in their lamps were not rebuked by the Bridegroom, but by the wise virgins.

When the foolish virgins returned from the dealer they found the door shut. The words, "I do not know you," mean He knew them not as among the invited guests. Simple courtesy had demanded that all invited guests should be ready whenever the Bridegroom was announced, no matter how late or early. His refusal to their, "Lord, open (the door) to us," was occasioned by two things. He could not see who was outside and there would be interruption of the ceremony, should He or any other guest open the door, when greetings would have to be extended to the late comers. The shut door was for privacy as was the Oriental custom during a marriage.

What happened to the foolish virgins? The answer is found in Luke 32:35-38. "Let your loins be girded about you and your lights shining and ye yourselves like unto men that wait for their Lord, when he will return from the wedding: that when he cometh and knocketh, they may open unto him immediately, and if he cometh to the second watch, or come in the third watch, and find them so, blessed are those servants."

These seem to be the "foolish virgins" for the following reasons: their loins are girded. They are awake and ready. They have oil and their lamps are burning. They have learned their lesson and are waiting for their Lord, "when he will return from the wedding." When they hear the knock to announce His arrival they will open the door at once. We are not told how much the "foolish" lose and the "wise" gain. The warning is that only half will be prepared to enter into the full eminence of the marriage.

We may conclude that the virgins who had no oil lacked something symbolized by oil in their lamps. In the Old Testament, the anointing by oil symbolized the presence of God. For example, Jacob anointed with oil the stone he had used for his pillar and called the place Beth-el. (Gen. 29:18) When Samuel anointed David with oil, "the Spirit of the Lord came upon David from that day forward." (I Sam. 16:13) Paul addressing Christians said, "Know ye not that ye are the temple of God, and that the Spirit of God dwelleth within you?" (I Cor. 3:16)

The first verse in Matthew 25 states that the kingdom of heaven shall be "likened to ten virgins," indicating that heaven will have within it all "ten virgins," both the wise and the foolish who could not enter the marriage feast. In like manner there will be Christians who will not be allowed to attend the marriage ceremony at the Second Advent. However, since the parable is addressed to all Christians, all are given a chance to profit by it. Those who do not do so have only themselves to blame. "Watch, therefore, for ye know neither the day nor the hour wherein the Son of man cometh." (Matt. 25:13)

Parable Two: The Talents

Matthew 25 tells of the parable of the Talents. "For the kingdom of heaven is as a man travelling into a far country, who called his own servants, and delivered unto them his goods. And unto one he gave five talents, to another two, and to another one; to every man according to his several ability; and straightway took his journey. Then he that had received the five talents went and traded with the same and made them other five talents. And likewise he that had received two, he also other two. But he that had received one went and digged in the earth and hid his Lord's money." (vs. 14-18)

As in the first parable, this parable applies only to Christians who are the Lord's own servants. Matthew continues, "After a long time the Lord of those servants cometh and reckoned with them. And so he that had received five talents came and brought other five talents. He also that had received two talents came and said, Lord, thou deliveredst unto me two talents: behold, I have gained two other talents besides them...Then he which had received the one talent came and said, Lord I knew thee that thou art an hard man reaping where thou hast not sown, and gathering where thou hast not strawed: And I was afraid, and went and hid thy talent in the earth: lo, there thou hast that is thine." (vs. 19-20, 22, 24-25)

Those who had made good use of their talents the Lord praised, saying, "Well done, thou good and faithful servant. (v. 23) But the one who did nothing but hide the money in the ground, was judged by his own standard. Not only was his talent taken away, but he was himself cast, "into outer darkness." Similar judgments are to be found in Paul's epistles. Writing to the Christians in

Rome, Paul said, "...we shall all stand before the judgment seat of Christ...then every one of us shall give account of himself to God." (Rom. 14:10, 14) To the Corinthians he wrote, "for we must all appear before the judgment seat of Christ; that every one may receive the things done in his body, according to that he hath done, whether it be good or bad." (II Cor. 5:10)

In his first epistle to the Corinthians Paul wrote, "...Every man shall receive his own reward according to his labour. For we are all labourers together with God." (I Cor. 3:9) After saying that our labors must be founded in Christ, he adds, "If any man's work abide which he hath thereupon he shall receive a reward. If any man's work shall be burned, he shall suffer loss; but he himself shall be saved." (I Cor. 3:14-15) It is clear from this statement that the judgment seat of Christ does not affect the question of salvation which depends solely on our faith. It is concerned only with an assessment of what we have made in this life of the talents and opportunities given to us, and on this will depend our future position in the kingdom of God.

The Kingdom Come

We are not given in the Scriptures all the details of this wonderful moment of future history when, "For the Lord himself shall descend from heaven with a shout, with the voice of the archangel, and with the trump of God: and the dead in Christ shall rise first." (I Thess. 4:16) *The Rapture*

When Jesus Christ came on earth as a lonely Galilean, He preached the Gospel of the Kingdom and revealed in parables, in mighty sayings, in mighty deeds, the glory and power of His coming kingdom. In doing for a few, (miracles) He showed what He will do for all when the light of His kingdom shall cover the earth as the waters now fill the seas. He did not heal all the sick, the blind and the lame. His ministry was only a foreshadowing of His mighty work of restoration, reserved for the kingdom age which will come with the Second Advent. He chose only twelve disciples to whom He gave power over all manner of sickness, disease and over demons, to demonstrate His power.

One common thought prevalent in our day of grace is the conversion of the world and the salvation of as many as possible. The real truth is that entire age of the Lord has been set aside by God to, "take out a people for His name," (Acts 25:14) as a people being prepared to reign with Him in His kingdom. "For many are called, but few are chosen." (Matt. 22:14)

The Second Advent of Christ will mark the end of our present 'Age of the Lord' (grace) and the First Resurrection, when the dead 'in Christ' (the overcomers) will appear on earth. "Blessed and holy is he that hath part in the first resurrection; on such the second death hath no power, but they shall be priests of God and of Christ, and shall reign with him a thousand years." (Rev. 20:6)

Many Christians are looking, longing and waiting for the kingdom of God to come, when all sin and pain and sorrow from this earth shall pass away and they will meet their loved ones. This is what has been taught and what they want to believe. But a reunion with loved ones at that time cannot be found in the Scriptures. The truth is as found in Rev. 20:5, "But the rest of the dead live not again until the thousand years were finished." The dead would include millions who will only be resurrected at the end of the thousand years as reported by John, the Revelator.

It is most regrettable that ministers of the Gospel for century after century, with few exceptions, have failed to differentiate between the thousand year kingdom age and the "age of ages," which in Eph. 1:10 is called the "dispensation of the fullness of time," and with its end, time is no more. (eternity) Scripture dealing with the end of the ages is often attributed to the age of the Lord. (Kingdom age)

Only after the coming thousand year kingdom age, "And I saw the dead, small and great stand before God: and the books were opened: and another book was opened, which is the book of life: and the dead were judged out of those things which were written in the books, according to their works." (Rev. 20:12) "And death and hell were cast into the lake of fire. This is the Second death. And whosoever was not found written in the book of life was cast into the lake of fire." (Rev. 20:14-15)

There is a gross misunderstanding by almost all Bible readers concerning the "lake of fire." This author presents the works of Charles H. Prigeon, M.A., (Is Hell Eternal) that correctly explains the lake of fire and brimstone: "The lake of fire and brimstone signifies a fire burning with brimstone. The word, 'brimstone' or sulphur defines the character of the fire. The word, 'theion' (Greek) translated brimstone, is exactly the same word, 'theion' which means divine."

"Sulphur, or brimstone, was sacred to the deity among the ancient Greeks and was used to fumigate, to purify, and to cleanse and to consecrate to the deity: for this purpose they burned it in their incense...The verb derived from 'theion' is 'theioo,' which means to hallow, to make divine, or to dedicate to a god." (See Liddell and Scott Greek English Lexicon, 1897 Edition)

"To any Greek, or to any trained in the Greek language, 'a lake of fire and brimstone' would mean 'a lake of divine purification.' The idea of judgment need not be excluded. Divine "purification' and divine 'consecration' are the plain meaning in ancient Greek. In the ordinary explanation this fundamental meaning of the word is entirely left out, and nothing but 'eternal torment' is associated with it."

"Every man's work shall be made manifest; for the day shall declare it, because it shall be revealed by fire; and the fire shall try every man's work of what worth it is. If any man's work abide which he hath built thereupon, he shall receive a reward. If any man's work shall be burned, he shall suffer loss: but he himself shall be saved; yet so as by fire." (I Cor. 3:13-15) The Ferrar Fenton Bible plainly states it is a 'divine fire' as used in Rev. 19:21, 20:10, and 21:9.

Another Greek word that is often translated incorrectly is, "aion" which literally means 'age' or a period of time. (Young's Literal) It has been translated into fifteen different words and phrases in the King James Version of the New Testament. Examples are, world, never, world without end, word began, eternal, forever for evermore, never, etc. In every case the words are taken from a single word, "aion" and should only be translated, "age." An age has a beginning and an end. That which is eternal is timeless. The Bible does not use any word that is equivalent to our English word eternal.

It should be pointed out that although the King James Version of the Bible is a magnificent work, only the original writings of the apostles and prophets are inspired, not any of the translations. That is why we have concordances like Young and Strong and Greek-English lexicons to correct errors in translations. An example is found in Matt. 25:46 which reads, "And these shall go away into everlasting punishment but the righteous into life eternal." Young's Literal, Ferrar Fenton, Concordant Literal N.T. reads that the "sinner goes into a long correction."

G. Campbell Morgan, D.D. pastor of the Moody Bible Institute wrote: "Let me say to Bible students that we must be very careful how we use the word, 'eternity.' There is no word in the whole book of God corresponding with the word, eternity, which as commonly used among us, means absolutely without end." If age which has time is translated eternal, one immediately gets the wrong idea. The common thought seems to have been that any age following this present age must be identical with eternity, which is gross error.

The word "torment" also needs study. In the New Testament the same word is used of one, "sick of the palsy" grievously "tormented." (Matt. 8:61) It is used of the disciples ship in Galilee, and is translated "tossed with the waves." (Matt. 14:24) It is translated by the word "vexed," in speaking of Lot. (II Peter 2:8) It is translated by a word that means "birth-pains." (Rev. 12:8) In other scriptures it is translated by the word torment or tormented. The original idea of the verb is, "to put to the test by rubbing on a touchstone." Then it means to question by applying some test or torture to discover whether true or not. The original idea was to test some metal that looked like gold to find whether it was real or not.

The meaning and usage of the word torment harmonizes with the idea of the divine purification and the torment is the test to find whether there has been any change in the sufferer or not. Through the hidden, loving purpose of God, every pang of torment will be a birth-pang; "Behold, I am making all things new." (literal) He will leave no part in the universe unrenewed. "Every knee shall bow and every tongue...confess" (Phil. 2:10-11, literal) The ages of the ages come to an end. "Than cometh the end." (I Cor. 15:24-28) Time ceases...There will be no, "day and night" in eternity. The suffering lasts only while there is, "day and night." (Rev. 20:10)

When the end of the ages of the ages is completed and time is no more, God will have completed the universal restitution of all things as He had spoken by the mouth to all His holy prophets since the world began. "That in the dispensation of the fullness of times he might gather together in one all things of Christ, both which are in heaven, and which are on earth; . . . (Ephesians 1:10)

"And I saw a new heaven and a new earth, for the first heaven and the first earth were passed away; and there was no more sea. And I John saw the holy city, new Jerusalem, coming down from God out of heaven, prepared as a bride adorned for her husband. And I heard a great voice out of heaven saying, Behold, the tabernacle of God is with men, and he will dwell with them, and they shall be his people, and God himself shall be with them. and be their God. And God shall wipe away all tears from their eyes; and there shall be no more death, neither sorrow, not crying, neither shall there be any more pain: for the former things are passed away." (Rev. 21:1-4)

Epilogue

This study has examined Scriptural prophecies in the light of recorded history which reveal to us the magnitude of the impending changes which are about to come upon the world, the symptoms of which are as clear as can be. Indeed, the extreme urgency of these days is evidenced by the on-rushing tide of unprecedented upheaval throughout the world – political, economic, environmental, religious, etc. These in turn have created a state of utter confusion and violence everywhere. Whole communities, nations, kingdoms and countries have been thrown into unparalleled chaos of revolutionary destruction by "mob power" democracy gone haywire! Peace processes the world over, are falling apart in quick succession before our very eyes.

The sudden eruption of violence increases almost daily in Palestine and Jerusalem, with no obvious end in sight. It could easily spill over into a World War III scenario. No matter how reluctant the Arab nations are to become embroiled in another Middle East crisis, God will have the last word: "Behold the day of the Lord cometh...For I will gather all nations against Jerusalem to battle; and the city shall be taken, and the houses rifled, and the women ravished; and half of the city shall go forth into captivity, and the residue of the people shall not be cut off from the city. Then shall the Lord go forth against those nations, as when he fought in the day of battle. And his feet shall stand in that day upon the mount of Olives, which is before Jerusalem on the east and towards the west, and there shall be a very great valley; and half of the mountain shall remove toward the north, and half of it toward the south." (Zech. 14:1-4)

However, most students of Bible prophecy are aware that, according to the Scriptures a divine intervention at that time will settle forever the "Peace of Jerusalem." I also believe most students of the Scriptures are agreed on the close approach of the end of this age, (world order) and the consequently rapidly diminishing opportunity to mend their ways while there is yet time. Futurists and Historicists widely differ in their interpretation of prophecy, but it is the spirit of warning their readers, which urges them to take up their pens. The paths they choose may diverge widely but the goal they have in view is the same.

Unfulfilled prophecy may serve to warn us of coming events, but the fulfillment of other prophecies is first necessary to establish faith. Not only does this show that God can, and does, foretell the future, but it demonstrates that the course of history is under His control. He is able to perform His will and achieve His purposes in a way, and at a time which He has set centuries in advance. Consequently the exposition of fulfilled prophecy brings more glory to God than controversial speculations about future unfulfilled prophecy. We are told to watch because there are other prophecies to be fulfilled as the time approaches for our Lord to come. The last Sign of all will be the appearance in person of the Son of Man. Are you going to wait until that final sign is given before you believe? If you do, it will be too late!

* * * * * * * * *

"In that day a man shall cast his idols of silver, and take his idols of gold, which they make each one for himself to worship, to the moles and to the bats; To go into the clefts of the rock, for fear of the Lord, and for the glory of his majesty, when he ariseth to shake the earth. Cease ye from man, whose breath is he to be accounted of?" (Isaiah 2:20-22)

* * * * * * * * *

This study is an endeavor to rouse at least a few of our countrymen and women to a realization that, THE KINGDOM OF GOD IS AT HAND, even if they do not agree with the conclusions presented herein.   Full agreement can hardly be expected even as this author has ventured to disagree on certain points with other expositors of the Bible. The expectation that the Second Coming of our Lord is at hand, must become paramount in our thinking and calculations for the near future if we are to be ready for the fearful yet glorious appearing of our great God, Redeemer and Saviour, Jesus Christ

The End

E. Raymond Capt

APPENDIX

The Ten Lost Tribes of Israel

"The kingdom of Israel, which had lasted for two hundred years, had now come to an end, in 721 B.C., and members of the Ten Tribes who had been hurried off to Assyria became the, 'Lost Tribes,' for they have never again emerged in world history." So wrote Reader's Digest, "Story of the Bible World, 1959, p. 84. Is this a true statement of the facts?

Here is what Jewish theologians and authors say:

"The ten tribes (of Israel) have been absorbed among the nations of the world. We look forward to the gathering of all the tribes at some future day." (Chief Rabbi Rev. J. H. Hertz in a letter to Capt. Merton Smith, Nov. 18, 1916)

"Here's a paradox, a paradox, a most ingenious paradox: an anthropological fact, many Christians may have much more Hebrew-Israelite blood in their veins than most of their Jewish neighbors." (Alfred M. Lilienthal, Jr. - "What Price Israel," 1953 p. 223)

"Isaiah, the prophet wrote that the remnant of Yahweh's people would be found in the isles of the sea. Isn't it reasonable this remnant may be the people of the British Isles...These were the fellows who emigrated to the next island and came to call themselves Scotsmen...Last but not least, consider that the word, 'Britain' may well be a corruption of the Hebrew, 'Brith-am,' meaning the people of the Covenant. What do I mean by all this? Simple, the Presbyterians, Baptists, Methodists, Episcopalians, and the Irish Catholics are really my cousins - all right, so its a few times removed. All of us knew it all along."

(Harry Golden – "Only in America" – Southwest Jewish Press, April 20, 1967)

"The most startling theory, however, is one which has sprung up within the last few years and which concerns the lost Israelites (ten tribes) not in any distant, romantic people, but in the prosaic Englishmen who are literally our neighbors. The theory seems to be gaining ground. Meetings are constantly held; and there is scarcely a town of importance in this country (England) which does not contain some persons who earnestly believe in its truth." (Jewish Chronicle, May 2, 1879)

...Wherefore there are but two tribes in Asia and Europe subject to the Romans, while the ten tribes are beyond the Euphrates till now, and are an immense multitude, and not to be estimated by numbers." (Flavius Josephus, "Antiquities of the Jews," Book XI, Chapter V, v.2)

"if the ten tribes have disappeared, the literal fulfillment of the prophecies would be impossible; if they have not disappeared, obviously they must exist under a different name." (The Jewish Encyclopedia, Vol. XII, 1905, p. 249)

"Historically the Northern Israelites had been exiled from the land of Israel by the Assurance. They did become part of the Scythian-Cimmerian and Gothic hosts and did ultimately settle in northwest Europe and the British Isles...it also seems certain that wherever else the Lost Ten Tribes of Israel may be, the overwhelming majority of them are to be found within these nations...Ezekiel did foresee, (Eze. 37:16-28) Judah, and... the children of Israel his companions being re-united with Joseph (represented by the stick of Ephraim) and all the house of Israel his companions. (Yair Davidy, "The Tribes," Russel-Davis Pub. Hebron, Israel, 1994, p.447)

Here is what our Founding Fathers, and authors of the period say:

"I felt on his (George Washington's) death, with my countrymen that verily a great man hath fallen this day in Israel."

(Writings of Thomas Jefferson, Jefferson Memorial Assoc., Vol. XIV, 1907, p.52)

"Now, as my soul liveth, and as I liveth who hath made me a ruler in Israel." (Sir Walter Scott and Oliver Cromwell using these words, Woodstock, 1831, p. 387)

"That God would...guide our affairs in the dark and difficult Day: and make known what Israel ought to do...that He would confirm and increase Union and Harmony in the Colonies and throughout America." (Governor Jonathan Trumbull, Thanksgiving Proclamation, Nov. 16, 1775)

"These good people (first settlers of Plymouth, Mass.) were now satisfied, they had as plain a command of Heaven to attempt a removal (from England, Ireland and Scotland), as ever their father Abraham had for his leaving the Chaldean territories...But whilst he (John Winthrop) thus did, as our New English Nehemiah, the part of a ruler in managing the public affairs of our American Jerusalem...he made himself still an exacter parallel unto the governor of Israel." (Pastor Cotton Mather, Magnalia Christi Americana. Vol. I, 1620, p.46)

"God will humble me before the sun, and in the sight of all Israel." (Pastor Jonathan Michell, Quote by Cotton Mather, Ecclesiastical History, Vol. II, 1702, p.89)

"The promises made to Abraham, to Isaac, and to Jacob, all fulfilled in the Anglo-Saxon Race." (E.P. Ingersoll, Lost Israel Found, Topeka, Kansas Publishing House, 1886)

"Then oh, you people of Israel gather together as one Man, and together as one Tree...And you Seed of Israel both lesse and more, the rattling of your dead bones together is at hand. Sinews, Flesh and Life: at the Word of Christ it comes"...(Edward Johnson, Historian, Working Providences of Sions's Saviour in New England, Charles Scribner, 1910, p.60)

Here is what the Scriptures say:

"James, a servant of God and of the Lord Jesus Christ, to the twelve tribes which are scattered abroad, greetings." (James 1:1)

"Hath God cast away his people...God hath not cast away his people which he foreknew." (Romans 11:1-2)

"And he shall set up an ensign for the nations, and shall assemble together the outcasts of Israel, and gather together the dispersed of Judah from the four corners of the earth." (Isaiah 11:12)

"Moreover, I will appoint a place for my people Israel, and will plant them, that they may dwell in a place of their own, and move no more: neither shall the children of wickedness afflict them any more, as beforetime." (II Sam. 7:10)

"That in blessing I will bless thee, and in multiplying I will multiply thy seed as the stars of the heavens, and as the sand which is upon the sea shore..." (Gen. 22:17, God to Abraham)

"I will perform the oath which I sware unto Abraham thy father: And I will make thy seed as to multiply as the stars of heaven, and will unto thy seed all these countries: and in thy seed shall all the nations of the earth be blessed." (Gen. 26:3-4, God to Isaac)

"And thy seed shall be as the dust of the earth, and thou shalt spread abroad to the west, and to the east, and to the north, and to the south: and in thee and in thy seed shall all the families of the earth be blessed." (Gen. 28:14, God to Jacob)

"...for this is the firstborn: put thy right hand upon his head. And his father refused, and said, I know it, I know it my son, I know it: he also shall become a people, and he shall be great: but truly his younger brother shall be greater than he, and his seed shall become a multitude of nations." (Gen 48:18-20, Jacob to Joseph)

"...and I will establish the throne of his kingdom over Israel for ever." (I Chron. 22:10, God to David)

"If they break my statutes, and keep not my commandments: Then I will visit their transgression with the rod, and their iniquity with stripes. Nevertheless my lovingkindness will I not utterly take from him, nor suffer my faithfulness to fail. My covenant will I not break, nor alter the thing that is gone out of my lips. Once I have sworn by my holiness that I will not lie unto David. His seed shall endure for ever as the sun before me. It shall be established for ever as the moon, and as a faithful witness in heaven, Selah." (Psalm 89:31-37, God to David)

The Marks of Israel

How strange it is, that with all the definite and positive assurances in the Word of God as to Israel's continuance forever as a Nation, there has never been any continued or persistent effort on the part of genuine Bible believers to find them. That they have been content to let them fade away and vanish into nothingness is surely a deep reproach on all true Christians.

There is, however, one probable explanation. It was GOD'S WILL AND PURPOSE TO HIDE THEM. While the Jews (some of whom are only a part of the House of Judah) occupied the stage, and even called themselves, "Israel," God could work unhindered with and in, "Lost Israel," till He had finished His predetermined work and without them knowing they were the people of the Book. Only as Israel's time of punishment had run out, with the whole of God's purposes at the point of complete fulfillment, was the identity of Israel to become known.

However, it is a matter of inspired record that God placed "marks" on His people Israel. During the Christian dispensation, Lost Israel was to possess these marks of identification. So then, if we can discover the nations and people with Israel's marks, we have found the people whom God chose to serve Him and be a channel of blessing to all mankind. The God-given marks are very many, and while the following list is not exhaustive, they constitute a chain of evidence utterly impossible to ignore.

One race, and one race alone, has all these marks. Nations within this race may have only a portion of them, but there is a race as a whole that has them all. With a few exceptions, Joseph (the birthright nation) was the recipient of them all. By inheritance, his two sons, Ephraim (Great Britain and the commonwealth nations) and Manasseh (U.S.A.) will be found possessing them all.

While Israelites remain in other countries, the United States is home to millions of all the thirteen tribes (One out of many) and thus is representative of the whole House of Jacob. We are bound by Israel's responsibilities, fulfilling Israel's destiny. The MARKS are on us everywhere; in our name; in our Sabbath; in our Institutions; in our Philanthropy; in our Commerce; in our Wealth; in our Mines; in our Agriculture, in our Churches; in our Missionary enterprises; in our Armed forces; in our Possession of the Bible, all birthmarks which neither time, nor the ages, nor even our sins can wipe out.

The Marks of Israel

1. Israel to be a great and mighty nation.
   Gen. 12:2; 18:18; Deut. 4:7, 8.
2. Israel to have multitudinous seed.
   Gen. 13:16; 15:5; 22:17; 24:60; 24; 28:3; 14; 32:12;
   49:22; Isa. 10:22; Hos. 1:10; Zech. 10:7, 8.
3. Israel to spread abroad to the West, East, North and South.
   Gen. 28:14; Isa. 42:5, 6.
4. Israel to have a new home.
   II Sam. 7:10; I Chron. 17:9.
5. Israel's home to be north-west of Palestine.
   Isa. 49:12; Jer. 3:18.
6. Israel to live in islands and coasts of the earth.
   Isa. 41:1; 49:1-3; 51:5; Jer. 31:7-10.
7. Israel to become a company of nations.
   Gen. 17:4-6, 15, 16; 35:11; 48:19; Eph. 2:12.
8. Israel to have a Davidic King (a perpetual monarchy within Israel). II Sam. 7:13, 19; I Chron. 22:10; II Chron. 13:5; Psa. 89:20, 37; Eze. 37:24; Jer. 33:17, 21, 26.
9. Israel to colonize and spread abroad.
   Gen. 28:14; 49:22; Deut. 32:8; 33:17; Psa. 2:8; Isa. 26:15;
   27:6; 54:2; Zech. 10:8, 9.

10. Israel to colonize the desolate place of the earth.
    Isa. 35:1; 43:19, 20; 49:8; 54:3; 58:11, 12.
11. Israel to lose a colony, then expand, demanding more room.
    Isa. 49:19, 20.
12. Israel to have all the land needed.
    Deut. 32:8.
13. Israel to be the first among the nations.
    Gen. 27:29; 28:13; Jer. 31:7.
14. Israel to continue as a nation for ever.
    II Sam. 7:16, 24, 29; I Chron. 17:22-27; Jer. 31:35-37.
15. Israel's home to be invincible by outside forces.
    II Sam. 7:10; Isa. 41:11-14.
16. Israel to be undefeatable - defended by God.
    Num. 24:8, 9; Isa. 15-17; Micah 5:8, 9.
17. Israel to be God's instruments in destroying evil.
    Jer. 51:20; 51:19-24; Dan. 2:34, 35.
18. Israel to have a land of great mineral wealth.
    Gen. 49:25, 26; Deut. 8:9; 33:15-19.
19. Israel to have a land of great agricultural wealth.
    Gen. 27:28; Deut. 8:7, 9; 28:11; 33:13, 14, 28.
20. Israel to be rich by trading.
    Isa. 60:5-11; 61:6.
21. Israel to be envied and feared by all nations.
    Deut. 2:25; 4:8, 28:10; Isa. 43:4; 60:10, 12; Micah 7:16, 17; Jer. 33:9.
22. Israel to lend to other nations, borrowing of none.
    Deut. 15:6; 28:12.
23. Israel to have a new name.
    Isa. 62:2; 65:15; Hos. 2:17.
24. Israel to have a new language.
    Isa. 28:11 (The Bible, by means of which God speaks now to Israel, is English not Hebrew).
25. Israel to possess the gates of his enemies.
    Gen. 22:17.
26. Israel to find the aborigines diminishing before them.
    Deut. 33:17; Isa. 60:12; Jer. 31:7-10.

27. Israel to have control of the seas.
Deut. 33:19; Num. 24:7; Psa. 89:25; Isa. 60:5 (F. Fenton translates this last, "when rolls up to you all the wealth of the sea". That could not be unless Israel controlled it).

28. Israel to have a new religion (New Covenant).
Heb. 8:10-13; 9:17; Matt. 10:5-7; Luke 1:77; 2:32; 22:20; John 11:49-52; Gal. 3:13.

29. Israel to lose all trace of her lineage.
Isa. 42:16-19; Hos. 1:9, 10; 2:6; Rom. 11:25.

30. Israel to keep Sabbath for ever (one day in seven set aside).
Ex. 31:13, 16, 17; Isa. 58:13, 14.

31. Israel to be called the sons of God (i.e., accept Christianity).
Hos. 1:10-11.

32. Israel to be a people saved by the Lord.
Deut. 33:27-29; Isa. 41:8-14; 43:1-8; 44:1-3; 49:25, 26; 52:1-12; 55:3-10, 13; Jer. 46:27, 28; Eze. 34:10-16; Hos. 2:23; 13:9-14; 14:4, 6.

33. Israel to be the custodians of the Oracles (Scriptures) of God.
Psa. 147:19, 21; Isa. 59:21.

34. Israel to carry the Gospel to all the world.
Gen. 28:14; Isa. 43:10-12 (witnesses), 21; Micah 5:7.

35. Israel to be kind to the poor and set slaves free.
Deut. 15:7, 11; Psa. 72:4; Isa. 42:7; 49:9; 58:6.

36. Israel to be the heir of the world.
Rom. 4:13.

37. Israel to be God's Glory.
Isa. 46:13; 49:3; 60:1, 2.

38. Israel to possess God's Holy Spirit as well as His Word.
Isa. 44:3; 59:21; Hagg. 2:5.

39. Israel to be God's Heritage, formed by God, for ever.
Deut. 4:20; 7:6; 14:2; II Sam. 7:23; I Kings 8:51, 53; Isa. 43:21; 54:5-10; Hos. 2:19, 23; Joel 2:27; Micah 7:14-18.

40. Israel to the nation appointed to bring glory to God.
Isa. 41:8-16; 43:10, 21; 44:23; 49:3.

"Hearken to me, ye that follow after righteousness, ye that seek the Lord: Look unto the rock whence ye are hewn, and to the hole of the pit whence ye are digged. Look unto Abraham, your father, and unto Sarah that bear you: for I called him alone, and blessed him, and increased him . . . . Hearken unto me, my people; and give ear unto me, O my nation."

Isaiah 51:1-3, 4

"YE SEED OF ISRAEL'S CHOSEN RACE,
YE RANSOMED OF THE FALL,
HAIL HIM WHO SAVES YOU BY HIS GRACE,
AND CROWN HIM LORD OF ALL."